BAPTISTWAYPRESS®

Adult Bible Teaching Guide

The Gospel of Mark

Jesus' Works and Words

James Carter
David Morgan
Bobby Bragg
Travis Bundrick
Emily Martin

BAPTISTWAYPRESS®

Dallas, Texas

The Gospel of Mark: Jesus' Works and Words—Adult Bible Teaching Guide
Copyright © 2007 by BAPTISTWAY PRESS®.
All rights reserved.
Printed in the United States of America.

No part of this book may be used or reproduced in any manner whatsoever without written permission except in the case of brief quotations. For information, contact BAPTISTWAY PRESS, Baptist General Convention of Texas, 333 North Washington, Dallas, TX 75246–1798.

BAPTISTWAY PRESS® is registered in U.S. Patent and Trademark Office.

Scripture marked NIV is taken from The Holy Bible, New International Version (North American Edition), copyright © 1973, 1978, 1984 by the International Bible Society. Used by permission of Zondervan Publishing House. Unless otherwise indicated, all Scripture quotations in lessons 1-7 and on the back cover are from the New International Version.

Scripture marked NASB is taken from the New American Standard Bible®, Copyright © The Lockman Foundation 1960, 1962, 1963, 1968, 1971, 1972, 1973, 1975, 1977, 1995. Used by permission. Unless otherwise indicated, all Scripture quotations in lessons 8-13 and the Christmas lesson are from the New American Standard Bible.

Scripture marked NRSV is taken from the New Revised Standard Version Bible, copyright 1989, Division of Christian Education of the National Council of the Churches of Christ in the United States of America. Used by permission. All rights reserved.

BAPTISTWAY PRESS® Management Team
Executive Director, Baptist General Convention of Texas: Charles Wade
Director, Missions, Evangelism, and Ministry Team: Wayne Shuffield
Ministry Team Leader: Phil Miller
Publisher, BAPTISTWAY PRESS®: Ross West

Cover and Interior Design and Production: Desktop Miracles, Inc.
Printing: Data Reproductions Corporation
Cover Photo: The Sea of Galilee, istockphoto.com

First edition: December 2007
ISBN: 1–931060–98–3

How to Make the Best Use of This Teaching Guide

Leading a class in studying the Bible is a sacred trust. This *Teaching Guide* has been prepared to help you as you give your best to this important task.

In each lesson, you will find first "Bible Comments" for teachers, to aid you in your study and preparation. The three sections of "Bible Comments" are "Understanding the Context," "Interpreting the Scriptures," and "Focusing on the Meaning." "Understanding the Context" provides a summary overview of the entire background passage that also sets the passage in the context of the Bible book being studied. "Interpreting the Scriptures" provides verse-by-verse comments on the focal passage. "Focusing on the Meaning" offers help with the meaning and application of the focal text.

The second main part of each lesson is "Teaching Plans." You'll find two complete teaching plans in this section. The first is called "Teaching Plan—Varied Learning Activities," and the second is called "Teaching Plan—Lecture and Questions." Choose the plan that best fits your class and your style of teaching. You may also use and adapt ideas from both. Each plan is intended to be practical, helpful, and immediately useful as you prepare to teach.

The major headings in each teaching plan are intended to help you sequence how you teach so as to follow the flow of how people tend to learn. The first major heading, "Connect with Life," provides ideas that will help you begin the class session where your class is and draw your class into the study. The second major heading, "Guide Bible Study," offers suggestions for helping your class engage the Scriptures actively and develop a greater understanding of this portion of the Bible's message. The third major heading, "Encourage Application," is meant to help participants focus on how to respond with their lives to this message.

As you begin the study with your class, be sure to find a way to help your class know the date on which each lesson will be studied. You might use one or more of the following methods:

- In the first session of the study, briefly overview the study by identifying with your class the date on which each lesson will be studied. Lead your class to write the date in the table of contents in their *Study Guides* and on the first page of each lesson.
- Make and post a chart that indicates the date on which each lesson will be studied.
- If all of your class has e-mail, send them an e-mail with the dates the lessons will be studied.
- Provide a bookmark with the lesson dates. You may want to include information about your church and then use the bookmark as an outreach tool, too.
- Develop a sticker with the lesson dates, and place it on the table of contents or on the back cover.

Note: A Christmas lesson is included. If your class uses the Christmas lesson, you may need to decide how to study the other lessons, such as by combining two lessons or studying the missed lesson at a special class meeting.

Here are some steps you can take to help you prepare well to teach each lesson and save time in doing so:

1. Start early in the week before your class meets.

2. If your church's adult Bible study teachers meet for lesson overview and preparation, plan to participate. If your church's adult Bible study teachers don't have this planning time now, look for ways to begin. You, your fellow teachers, and your church will benefit from this mutual encouragement and preparation.

3. Overview the study in the *Study Guide*. Look at the table of contents, and see where this lesson fits in the overall study. Then read or review the study introduction to the book that is being studied.

4. Consider carefully the suggested Main Idea, Question to Explore, and Teaching Aim. These can help you discover the main thrust of this particular lesson.

5. Use your Bible to read and consider prayerfully the Scripture passages for the lesson. Using your Bible in your study and in the class session can provide a positive model to class members to use their own Bibles and give more attention to Bible study themselves. (Each

writer of the Bible comments in both the *Teaching Guide* and the *Study Guide* has chosen a favorite translation. You're free to use the Bible translation you prefer and compare it with the translations chosen, of course.)

6. After reading all the Scripture passages in your Bible, then read the Bible comments in the *Study Guide*. The Bible comments are intended to be an aid to your study of the Bible. Read also the small articles—"sidebars"—in each lesson. They are intended to provide additional, enrichment information and inspiration and to encourage thought and application. Try to answer for yourself the questions included in each lesson. They're intended to encourage further thought and application, and you can also use them in the class session itself. Continue your Bible study with the aid of the Bible comments included in this *Teaching Guide*.

7. Review the "Teaching Plans" in this *Teaching Guide*. Consider how these suggestions would help you teach this Bible passage in your class to accomplish the teaching aim.

8. Consider prayerfully the needs of your class, and think about how to teach so you can help your class learn best.

9. Develop and follow a lesson plan based on the suggestions in this *Teaching Guide*, with alterations as needed for your class.

10. Enjoy leading your class in discovering the meaning of the Scripture passages and in applying these passages to their lives.

FREE! Additional adult Bible study comments by Dr. Jim Denison, pastor of Park Cities Baptist Church, Dallas, Texas, are online at www.baptistwaypress.org and can be downloaded free. These lessons are posted on the internet a week in advance of the first Sunday of use.

FREE! Downloadable teaching resource items for use in your class are available at www.baptistwaypress.org! Watch for them in "Teaching Plans" for each lesson. Then go online to www.baptistwaypress.org and click on "Teaching Resource Items" for this study. These items are selected from "Teaching Plans." They are provided online to make lesson preparation easier for hand-outs and similar items. Permission is granted to download these teaching resource items, print them out, copy them as needed, and use them in your class.

ALSO FREE! An additional teaching plan is available each week at www.baptistwaypress.org.

IN ADDITION: Enrichment teaching help is provided in the internet edition of the *Baptist Standard*. Access the ***FREE*** internet information by checking the *Baptist Standard* website at www.baptiststandard.com. Call 214–630–4571 to begin your subscription to the printed edition of the *Baptist Standard*.

Writers of This Teaching Guide

James Carter wrote "Bible Comments" on lessons one through seven. Dr. Carter is retired as director of the Louisiana Baptist Convention Church-Minister Relations Division. A graduate of Louisiana College and of Southwestern Baptist Theological Seminary (M. Div., Ph. D.), he served as a pastor for more than thirty years, including a decade at University Baptist Church, Fort Worth, Texas.

David Morgan wrote "Bible Comments" on lessons eight through thirteen plus the Christmas lesson. Dr. Morgan serves as pastor of Trinity Baptist Church, Harker Heights, Texas, and is a veteran Bible study curriculum writer.

Bobby Bragg, the writer of "Teaching Plans" for lessons one through three plus the Christmas lesson, is associate pastor of discipleship, Broadmoor Baptist Church, Madison, Mississippi. He has served other churches in Kentucky, Georgia, and Tennessee.

Travis Bundrick wrote "Teaching Plans" for lessons four through seven. He serves as executive pastor, New Hope Baptist Church, Cedar Park, Texas. He has served in education and administration ministries for churches in Texas, Louisiana, Mississippi, and Tennessee.

Emily Martin wrote "Teaching Plans" for lessons eight through thirteen. She is a professional writer specializing in business and Christian communication. She holds both B.A. and M.B.A. degrees from Southern Methodist University and a Th.M. from Dallas Theological Seminary. She and her husband have a son in college and a daughter in high school, and they are members of Park Cities Baptist Church, Dallas, Texas.

The Gospel of Mark: Jesus' Works and Words

How to Make the Best Use of This Teaching Guide   3
Writers for This Teaching Guide   7

Date of Study

UNIT ONE
Good News Today

LESSON 1	_____	*Let Me Introduce Jesus* Mark 1:1–20	11
LESSON 2	_____	*A Faith Worth Acting On* Mark 2:1–12	22
LESSON 3	_____	*Live the Unbound Life* Mark 2:13–17, 23—3:6	31

UNIT TWO
Showing Who Jesus Is

LESSON 4	_____	*More Than Meets the Eye* Mark 4:21–34	41
LESSON 5	_____	*Jesus and Hopeless Situations* Mark 4:35—5:43	51
LESSON 6	_____	*When Cleanliness Is Not Next to Godliness* Mark 7:1–23	61
LESSON 7	_____	*There Are None So Blind* Mark 8:11–26	72

UNIT THREE

With Jesus on the Way to the Cross

LESSON 8	_____	*Not an Easy Way* Mark 8:27–38	81
LESSON 9	_____	*Me First* Mark 9:30–37	92
LESSON 10	_____	*Disciple = Servant* Mark 10:32–45	102
LESSON 11	_____	*Discipleship in Dangerous Times* Mark 13:1–13, 32–37	113
LESSON 12	_____	*Not Me* Mark 14:10–31	124
LESSON 13	_____	*The Worst and Best of Times* Mark 14:61b–64; 15:9–24, 37–41; 16:1–8	134
CHRISTMAS LESSON	_____	*Glory to God!* Luke 2:1–20	145

How to Order More Bible Study Materials   155

Focal Text
Mark 1:1–20

Background
Mark 1:1–20

Main Idea
Jesus, whose identity as Christ and Son of God was verified in many ways, came proclaiming God's good news and calling people to follow him.

Question to Explore
If we knew nothing about Jesus before reading this passage, what would it tell us about him?

Teaching Aim
To lead the class to state what this passage tells us about Jesus and the response it calls us to make

UNIT ONE

Good News Today

Lesson One

Let Me Introduce Jesus

BIBLE COMMENTS

Understanding the Context

The Gospel of Mark begins with an introduction to Jesus. Mark's Gospel is usually considered the first one written. Probably written from Rome, the date it was written is generally accepted as around 65 A.D. The Gospel was addressed to the Gentile world, especially the Romans.

John Mark, who was a missionary associate of both Paul and Peter, is recognized as the author. That the Gospel content is based on the preaching of Peter is also generally acknowledged.

The Gospel of Mark moves quickly. Without preliminary background, the Gospel of Mark plunges into the action and activity of Jesus. Mark presents more of the power of God in Jesus Christ by his acts than by his teaching. Miracles are more prominent than discourses. This Gospel introduces Jesus by what he did.

Whenever Jesus is introduced, a decision is demanded. No one meets Jesus and goes away without some type of decision. So today, Jesus calls us to follow him in faith and discipleship.

Interpreting the Scriptures

Approach (1:1)

Mark asserted that what he wrote was the "beginning" of the gospel about Jesus Christ.[1] This could be understood as simply the beginning, where the story started. Or, the beginning could well be understood as a title for the whole gospel. The gospel of Jesus Christ started with these events, but it did not end there.

Every word in this first verse of Mark's Gospel has meaning. The word "gospel" means *good news*. The English word "gospel" is from an Old English word that means *God's spiel* or *the story about God*. The gospel is the good news that God loved us so much that he became one of us in Jesus Christ. Jesus lived a sinless life. He died on the cross for our sins. He arose from the dead and ascended to heaven, where he sits at the right hand of God to make intercession for us. To believe in Jesus as Savior brings one into a saving relationship with God. This is truly good news.

Notice that the good news is about "Jesus Christ." "Jesus" is from the Greek translation of the Hebrew name *Joshua*. The name means *the salvation of God*. "Christ" means the *anointed one*. We know the title from the Hebrew concept of the Messiah, the one who was chosen and anointed by God. "Jesus" is his name. "Christ" is his title.

Mark further identified Jesus Christ as "the Son of God." In the terms of John 3:16, Jesus was God's "one and only Son" or the *only-one-of-a-kind Son* of God. Mark described Jesus as the One who came from God anointed with the power of God to do great works.

The opening words of Mark's Gospel can serve as both a title for the book and a declaration of what Jesus did in the world. God proclaimed his good news in Jesus Christ.

Announcement (1:2–8)

1:2–3. To show that Jesus came into the world in fulfillment of prophecy, the writer quoted two Old Testament passages of Scripture. Although Mark introduced the prophecies as the word of Isaiah, actually the first quotation is from Malachi. In ancient times people were not as careful with precise documentation as we are.

The quotation promises that a messenger will be sent ahead. The "I" in the passage obviously refers to God. God is the One who sent the messenger. "You" refers to Jesus. The responsibility of the messenger was to prepare for the coming of the Christ.

Verse 3, quoting from Isaiah 40:3, gives the message. The voice was of the one calling from "the desert." Being "in the desert" would put him outside the conventions and institutions of the time. He called on them to "prepare the way for the Lord." This designation identifies Jesus as "Lord." The word "Lord" indicates one who was above the others, the one to whom others answered. Jesus both fit and accepted the designation. The earliest Christian confession of faith was, "Jesus is Lord."

In making the path straight, those who responded to "the voice" would follow a practice that occurred when a king or ruler traveled. The road would be improved, with the curves straightened and the rough places and potholes filled before the ruler traveled over it.

That was the message: prepare for the coming of a notable Person sent from God. That Person was Jesus Christ, the Son of God.

1:4–8. John, whom we know as John the Baptist, or more specifically John the Baptizer, was the messenger. John did not preach in the synagogues or the temple in Jerusalem. His ministry was conducted in the desert, along the Jordan River in the Judean wilderness area.

John's practice was to baptize those people who repented of their sins. The baptism by total immersion symbolized the person's repentance of his or her sins and the cleansing of that individual. Repentance involves the recognition of sin, sorrow for that sin, and turning away from it. The word "repentance" indicates a turning. The immersion in water signified that the sins were cleansed, as though they were washed away.

People flocked to hear John preach and to receive baptism. The terms "whole Judean countryside" and "all the people of Jerusalem" show the overwhelming response to John's preaching.

In contrast to the official religious leaders, John was not dressed well, and neither did he eat well. John dressed simply, in a garment made of woven camel's hair girded with a leather belt. The diet consisted of what he could gather in the wilderness: wild honey and locusts.

What attracted people to John was his message. He proclaimed that he was just the forerunner. After him would come one who was more powerful than he. In fact, John asserted that he was not even worthy of helping the One to come to put on his shoes.

Then John made clear the difference in his ministry and the ministry of the Christ. John baptized with water. This baptism was symbolic, indicating repentance from sin. Jesus would baptize with the Holy Spirit. The water baptism was external. The baptism of the Holy Spirit would be internal. John was merely the servant; Jesus was the Son.

Approval (1:9–13)

1:9–11. Without giving any of Jesus' background, Mark simply stated that Jesus came from Nazareth to Judea for baptism by John. Jesus was from Nazareth, which was in the northern part of the nation of Israel. Judea was in the southern section of the country. Jesus traveled from Nazareth to the Jordan River in Judea where John baptized.

Since Jesus was sinless, his baptism did not signify repentance as did the baptism of the other subjects of John's baptism. Rather than indicating repentance, Jesus' baptism signified that he identified with the people to whom he ministered. By his incarnation Jesus took on humanity, showing that he was one of us. By his baptism he further showed that he was one of us.

God showed his approval of Jesus' action by the "voice" from heaven. When Jesus was baptized, all heaven broke loose. The heavens opened as though they were torn apart. The Holy Spirit descended on Jesus as a dove would have fluttered down upon him. Too, a voice from heaven declared God's approval.

The voice identified Jesus as God's Son. This identification tracked the identification of Jesus Christ as the Son of God given in Mark 1:1. That declaration shows both the acceptance and the approval of Jesus as the Son of God. Not only was Jesus identified as the Son of God, he was the Son whom God loved.

Too, God approved of what Jesus did. God asserted that he was "well pleased" with his Son Jesus. The Father was "well pleased" with Jesus' identification with sinning humans.

1:12–13. The Holy Spirit who descended on Jesus filling him with his power also directed his actions. Through the guidance of the Holy Spirit, Jesus went into the desert for forty days. Forty days and forty nights are frequent biblical expressions of a time period (see, for example, Exodus 24:18). The purpose of the desert sojourn was to determine the shape his ministry would take.

While in the desert, Jesus was tempted by Satan. Mark does not give the content of the temptations as do Matthew and Luke (Matthew 4:1–11;

Luke 4:1–13). Neither does Mark tell how Jesus turned back the temptations. Mark, though, states that Jesus "was with the wild animals...." The desert was a place of danger and desolation. Totally alone, Jesus was with the animals of the desert. But Jesus was not without help. Angels, messengers from God, attended to his needs in the temptation experience.

Action (1:14–15)

1:14. Jesus began his ministry immediately. Without giving any of the details of John the Baptizer's imprisonment, Mark timed the beginning of Jesus' public ministry with John's imprisonment. While the temptation experience was in the Judean desert, Jesus' public ministry began in Galilee, his home territory.

John the Baptizer's message was a stern warning about sin and its outcome. Jesus' message was good news, the good news about God. Jesus' message from God was good news: people could be reconciled to God and saved from their sin.

1:15. This verse presents a summary of Jesus' message. With the coming of Christ into the world, the time of God's decisive activity for human salvation had come. This was the opportune time, the right time, for God to act in Christ.

The "kingdom of God" refers to the rule of God in the human heart. When we think of "kingdom," we usually think of a territory. God's kingdom, instead, is internal rather than external.

The message of Jesus requires a response. To enter the kingdom of God one must "repent and believe." "Repent" means *to turn*. To "repent" is to *turn from your sin and turn to Jesus*. To "believe" is to *take Jesus at his word*, trusting in him for forgiveness and salvation. The focus of this belief is the gospel, "the good news" that God loves you, acts for you in Jesus Christ, and forgives you of your sin, receiving you as one of his own.

Appeal (1:16–20)

1:16–18. The Sea of Galilee is really more like a lake, eight miles by thirteen miles in size. As Jesus walked along the shore of the Sea of Galilee he saw two fishermen casting a net into the sea. Mark gave no indication of whether they had prior contact with Jesus.

Jesus appealed to the brothers, Simon and Andrew, to follow him. Notice the directness of the appeal. Jesus called them to follow him personally. With the appeal also came a promise. Jesus promised that he would make them "fishers of men." Their profession suggested the metaphor. Whereas they had been *fishers of fish*, Jesus would make them "fishers of men." They would bring people into the presence of the Christ.

Apparently with no hesitation, Simon and Andrew left their nets and followed Jesus. They would cast their lot with him.

1:19–20. A little farther along the seashore Jesus came upon another pair of brothers, James and John the sons of Zebedee. These fishermen were in a boat repairing their nets, which may have been damaged in that morning's fishing foray.

Again, Mark does not record any previous contact they may have had with Jesus. But they, too, must have known something about him.[2] The terms of the call are not recorded in the call of these brothers. But Jesus called them. They, too, responded immediately, leaving the boat with their father and the hired help. They followed Jesus. Jesus issued an appeal with a promise that was followed by obedience.

Focusing on the Meaning

The introduction to Jesus Christ leads to the definite conclusion that Jesus is truly the promised Deliverer from God. He is the *only-one-of-a-kind* Son of God who brings salvation from sin and new life.

The public ministry of Jesus was preceded by the ministry of John the Baptizer, who prepared the way for the ministry of Jesus. John preached a baptism that signified repentance from sin. The message of Jesus presented forgiveness from sin through repentance and faith in Christ. Jesus assured that the right time was upon us in his life, ministry, death, and resurrection. The rule of God in the human heart, the kingdom of God, was at hand with the coming of Christ. To enter God's kingdom one must repent of sin and believe in Jesus.

Jesus was baptized by John primarily to show Jesus' identification with the people he had come to save. A voice from heaven and the coming of the Holy Spirit upon him like a descending dove verified his identity. After a sojourn in the desert in which Jesus determined the nature of his ministry, he began his public ministry.

As with the first disciples, Jesus gives us a direct and personal call to follow him. We are to respond in obedience to that call. In the midst of our normal, daily tasks, Jesus calls us to follow him as he did the two pairs of brothers. Our response to his call should also be immediate and obedient.

TEACHING PLANS

Teaching Plan—Varied Learning Activities

Connect with Life

1. Enlist someone in advance to research the topic *How to introduce a person properly*. (The focus could be an individual introduction or the introduction of a speaker.) Have the person give the report as the class session begins. The report should provide a few points of a good introduction.(For example: provide the person's name; provide background information that would be meaningful to the other person or the audience; provide personal information that would build a relationship to the other person or the audience; if introducing a speaker, provide information that will show the speaker's special qualifications for speaking on the topic.)

2. After the report on introductions is given, give participants a piece of paper or a note card. Then instruct them to jot down some ideas for introducing to the class a person they know or a famous individual from the past or present. (Provide an example for doing this as part of your instructions.) Invite volunteers to share their introductions. After several have reported, point out that the title of the study is, "Let Me Introduce Jesus."

Guide Bible Study

3. Share with the group that today's study is the introduction of Jesus and his ministry by Mark. In advance, enlist someone to summarize "Introducing the Gospel of Mark" in the *Study Guide*. Call for this summary, and then provide any additional information that seems

helpful by using information in "Understanding the Context" in this *Teaching Guide*.

4. Then ask members to become television or radio investigative reporters and find the bullet points that Mark was presenting in the lesson today. Divide the group into four different groups to do this. If the group is small, let one or two people work on each report. Either serve as the "anchor" yourself for the radio/television report, or select someone to do so. The anchor should be prepared to guide the reports and to encourage further thought by using the questions in the *Study Guide*. The anchor should begin the report by setting the scene. Each group would then provide its report. (A copy of the group assignments can be downloaded in "Teaching Resource Items" for this study from www.baptistwaypress.org.) Here are the group assignments:

- Reporter 1 will report from the desert with John the Baptist, using Mark 1:1–8 and "Introducing Jesus" in the *Study Guide*. (A possible technique is to interview John the Baptist plus those who were present that day.)
- Reporter 2 will report on Jesus' baptism in the Jordan River, using Mark 1:9–11 and "The Mission" in the *Study Guide*. (A possible technique is to interview Jesus and John the Baptist.)
- Reporter 3 will report on Jesus' temptation experience, using Mark 1:12–13 and "The Trial" in the *Study Guide*. (A possible technique is to report on the meaning of the experience.)
- Reporter 4 will report on Jesus' preaching and the call of the disciples, using Mark 1:14–20 and "The Message and the Call" in the *Study Guide*. (A possible technique is to interview someone who heard Jesus preach and also the four fishermen and perhaps the father of James and John.)

5. After all the reports, the news anchor should return to each reporter and ask, *Who do you think the man Jesus is?* Summarize the responses.

Encourage Application

6. In closing, relate to the group that today we have investigated the beginning of Jesus Christ's life and ministry, one of the most exciting news stories in history. Ask, *Do you think if these events had occurred*

today they would make the nightly news? If so, would they be the lead story? How can we live our lives so Jesus can be the lead story for us and the people we meet?

7. Give each person in the group a note card. Instruct them to write, "How to Introduce Jesus," as the heading. Ask them to develop an outline of how they can introduce Jesus to someone.

8. Close with a prayer that each member in the group will be given the opportunity to introduce someone to the Jesus they know and love.

Teaching Plan—Lecture and Questions

Connect with Life

1. Begin by using the information in the introductory paragraphs in the lesson in the *Study Guide* about going to a movie. Invite the members to tell about specific movies or events they have attended that left them feeling that way. Explore with the members their reasons for disappointment.

2. State that today we are going to study one of the most action-packed stories in the Bible. It has prophecy, trips to the desert, a voice from God, suspense, and dedicated disciples. This story is the beginning of the life and ministry of Jesus Christ. Introduce the Gospel of Mark by using information in "Understanding the Context" in this *Teaching Guide* and "Introducing the Gospel of Mark" in the *Study Guide*.

Guide Bible Study

3. Use the information in the *Study Guide* under the heading "Introducing Jesus (1:1–8)" to explore how Mark began his Gospel. Invite someone to read aloud Mark 1:1–8. Ask the members what they think is different about Mark's introduction in contrast to that of Matthew and Luke (no stories of Jesus' birth, for one thing). Ask, *What are some of the key words or ideas in these verses? How do you feel about the way Jesus is presented as the "Son of God"?* Lead the class to consider the role of John the Baptist in introducing Jesus. Ask, *How*

do you think Jesus would be introduced to the world today if this were the beginning time for his life and ministry?

4. Using the information in "The Mission (1:9–11)" section in the *Study Guide*, help the class discover additional important elements about Jesus in these verses. Enlist someone to read Mark 1:9–11, and then call for comments. Explain the meaning of Jesus' baptism, and emphasize God's approval of Jesus as his Son.

5. Point out that the *Study Guide* under the heading, "The Trial (1:12–13)," suggests that Mark 1:12–13 contains six key elements of Jesus' temptation. Invite someone to read aloud Mark 1:12–13. Receive comments about the elements. Then refer to the elements mentioned in the *Study Guide*. As you explore the six elements, ask members what they think facing each of them would have been like.

6. Have someone read Mark 1:14–20 while half the class listens for Jesus' message and the other half listens for the events in Jesus' call to the first four disciples. Receive comments and add insights from "The Message and the Call (1:14–20)" in the lesson in the *Study Guide*. Use the following questions to explore the disciples' responses:

    - What do you think excited the disciples so much about Jesus that they decided to follow him?
    - What did it mean for these men to drop what they were doing and follow Jesus?
    - What priorities had to change in their lives to follow Jesus?

Encourage Application

7. Refer the class to "Implications and Actions" in the *Study Guide* to review the lesson. Ask participants how they think the start of Jesus' ministry might be different today from in the first century. State that the two times are different, but the message is the same. Invite comments about how what we learned about Jesus in this lesson could help us in introducing Jesus to people today. State that it is our turn and responsibility to introduce Jesus to the world.

8. Close with a prayer identifying people we know who need to be introduced to Jesus. Pray for strength, wisdom, courage, and love to introduce Jesus to someone during the coming week.

NOTES

1. Unless otherwise indicated, all Scripture quotations in lessons 1–7 are from the New International Version.
2. See Luke 5:1–11; John 1:35–42; see also Mark 10:28.

Focal Text
Mark 2:1–12

Background
Mark 2:1–12

Main Idea
Faith takes action in response to the authority of Jesus.

Question to Explore
Who are you most like in this incident in Jesus' ministry?

Teaching Aim
To lead the class to decide on at least one way they will act on their faith in Jesus

UNIT ONE

Good News Today

Lesson Two

A Faith Worth Acting On

BIBLE COMMENTS

Understanding the Context

After calling the two sets of brothers to follow him, Jesus continued to minister in Galilee. Galilee was the northern area of Israel. On the Sabbath he went to a synagogue in Capernaum, a town located on the northwest shore of the Sea of Galilee. It was the home of Simon Peter. As a visiting rabbi, Jesus taught in the synagogue. The people were amazed that he taught with authority. They were accustomed to the rabbis referring to others as authorities when they taught. Jesus taught with his own authority (Mark 1:21–22).

While there, Jesus exorcised an evil spirit from a man. Then at Peter's home he healed Peter's mother-in-law of a fever. News of what Jesus did spread, and soon many people were brought to him for healing and exorcism (1:23–34).

Early the next morning Jesus went to a solitary place to pray. When Peter found Jesus, he informed him that the people were searching for him. Then Jesus went throughout the area performing his threefold ministry of preaching, teaching, and healing (1:35–39).

Among those healed was a man with leprosy. The man appealed to Jesus' willingness to heal him. The man indicated that he knew Jesus had

22

the power to heal him if Jesus had the will to do it. Acting with compassion, Jesus healed the man. Upon healing the man Jesus instructed him to verify the healing with the priest and to keep silent about the healing. But he did not. The man spread the word far and wide. Jesus could not go into the towns then without being besieged by people. So he stayed in the more lonely areas. Yet the people still found him and flocked to him (1:40–45).

Interpreting the Scriptures

Crowd (2:1–2)

2:1. Continuing his ministry in Galilee, Jesus returned to Capernaum a few days after the healing of the leper. Notice that the people in the area "heard that he had come home." Capernaum apparently was the headquarters of Jesus' ministry in Galilee. Capernaum was the home of Simon Peter and Andrew, and Jesus may have made their home his base of operations. Obviously, Jesus was at home there, and the people were comfortable with his being there.

2:2. Hearing that Jesus was in Capernaum, the people converged on the place where he was. The house was totally filled.

To these people Jesus preached "the word." While the content of his preaching is not given, the reference is to the good news, the gospel, which Jesus had previously announced. In Mark 1:15 the message of Jesus is summarized: God's right time had occurred; people could know the rule of God in their lives; they were to turn from their sin and believe this good news.

Since Jesus had been ministering actively in Galilee—teaching, preaching, and healing—the people who crowded the house had some idea of what to expect from Jesus. The populace crowded into and around the house that day to hear him. Observe that Jesus was teaching in a home, not the synagogue.

Compulsion (2:3–5)

2:3. Among the crowd in and around the house where Jesus taught were some men who had a compulsion to get a friend into Jesus' presence. They already must have been aware of Jesus' power to heal. The passage does not record the number of men bringing their friend to Jesus. The passage simply states "some men." But since four men carried him and later lowered him through the roof, there had to have been at least four friends, and there could have been more than four.

The friends had a "paralytic" with them. The nature of his paralysis is not given, but that the man could not walk was evident. Four of his friends carried the man, apparently on a mat or a pallet, probably with each of the four men handling a corner of the mat.

2:4. When the men with the paralyzed friend reached the house where Jesus taught, they saw they could not get in the house to get their friend to Jesus. The house was so filled with people they blocked the way to Jesus. Enterprising people that they were, they went to the roof of the house and dug through the roof above Jesus.

Most Palestinian houses of that time consisted of one to four rooms with a courtyard. An outside stairway led to the roof. The roof was flat. It was constructed of poles, often saplings, laid across the space between the walls about three feet apart. Smaller branches or reeds were then woven between the poles. Dirt or mud was placed on top of that and tamped down. Often grass grew on the roof. To break through a roof of that construction was not difficult. Neither was it difficult to repair.

Likely when the debris from the roof showered down on the people, they moved back enough to give space in front of Jesus. Probably with a rope attached to each corner of the mat and a man holding each rope, the friends lowered the paralytic man through the roof to Jesus.

2:5. When the man descended on the mat, Jesus acted immediately. Jesus acknowledged the faith that brought the man to him. That faith could have been the faith of the friends that Jesus could heal the paralytic man if only he could get to Jesus. Or the paralytic could have been the person of faith who urged his friends to get him to Jesus. Perhaps it was both. Addressing the paralytic man, Jesus said, "Son, your sins are forgiven." Faith that Jesus both could and would effectively act was the basis for the forgiveness. "Son" is a term of endearment and does not necessarily indicate anything about the age of the man.

The thought of the people of that day was that sin and suffering were connected directly. To them, suffering, which would include paralysis, was the result of sin. When a person suffered a debilitating disease, the belief was that it was because he or she had sinned.

UNIT ONE: Good News Today

The pronouncement of forgiveness by Jesus brought healing to the man. Jesus assumed both the power and prerogative to forgive sin. Jesus could forgive a person of his sin, his wrongdoing. In doing that, Jesus showed he also had the power to heal the person of his disability. Forgiveness by Jesus is far-reaching and all-encompassing.

Controversy (2:6–7)

2:6. Some "teachers of the law" were among those present in the crowded house. Also called "scribes" (NRSV, NASB), they were considered to be experts on the Jewish law. Not only did they transcribe the law, but they also interpreted the law. In their teaching, they cited other authorities. The teaching of Jesus was contrasted to their teaching because he taught as one who had authority in himself.

These "teachers of the law" did not speak out when they saw Jesus heal the paralytic and pronounce his forgiveness. But they had thoughts about it. Mark wrote that they were "thinking to themselves."

2:7. Their thoughts were about why Jesus, whom they called in their thoughts "this fellow," would talk like that. They wondered why he would pronounce the man forgiven of his sin.

Their thoughts moved on from that question to an assertion that Jesus was blasphemous in making that statement. Blasphemy is irreverent, impious, profane speech about God. So serious was blasphemy that in the Old Testament it carried a death penalty (see Leviticus 24:14–16).

Then their thoughts progressed to the affirmation that only God can forgive sin. Sin is directed against God. So God alone has the power to forgive sin.

This is the first of five controversies between Jesus and the Jewish religious leaders as recorded in Mark's Gospel. When Jesus forgave the paralytic man's sins, he stirred up controversy with the Jewish religious teachers. They thought Jesus had assumed for himself the prerogative of God to forgive sin.

Conclusion (2:8–12)

2:8. Jesus knew what they were thinking. Mark does not necessarily imply that Jesus knew this through supernatural means. Jesus could have known it with his perceptiveness and insight. Probably they gave their thoughts away by the look on their faces.

Jesus asked them why they were thinking those things. Notice that he did not have to outline their thoughts to them. Both Jesus and the teachers of the law knew what he meant.

2:9. Jesus followed that question with another question that is almost in the form of a riddle. He asked whether it would be easier to say to someone his or her sins were forgiven or to tell the paralytic person to take up his mat and walk.

2:10–11. Jesus proved the spiritual by the physical. He showed he had the power and the authority to forgive sin. He showed he had that spiritual power and authority by healing the man physically.

Jesus referred to himself as "the Son of Man." In Mark's Gospel, Jesus used this title as a self-designation. He designated himself as the "Son of Man." Others might declare Jesus the "Son of God" as Mark did in Mark 1:1, but Jesus called himself the "Son of Man." The title could mean simply *man*, a person. The title also could have Messianic overtones. Thus, Jesus could call himself "the Son of Man" without calling up the images of the conquering Messiah who would deliver the nation.

Jesus told them he would prove to them that he had the authority to forgive sin. He did not usurp God's authority. Jesus instructed the paralytic to pick up his mat and walk.

2:12. The man did just as Jesus instructed him. This person had been carried to the house and lowered into the presence of Jesus in a crowd of people through the roof of the house. Now he stood up, picked up his mat, and walked! The former paralytic did this in the presence of all those there. It was not a secret miracle but a public healing of the man.

Those who were present were amazed. They praised God for what they saw. They also exclaimed, "We have never seen anything like this!" Indeed, they had not.

The man and his friends had acted on faith. Jesus healed the man of his paralysis and forgave his sin.

Focusing on the Meaning

While practicing his ministry in Galilee, Jesus made his headquarters in the town of Capernaum on the northwest shore of the Sea of Galilee. Crowds followed him.

At one time, he preached and taught in a house that was more than filled to capacity. Friends of a paralytic man, or perhaps the paralytic himself, or perhaps all of them, had faith that Jesus would heal him if the man could just meet him. Showing ingenuity and compulsion, the men dug through the roof of the house and lowered the man on a mat before Jesus. Jesus recognized and commented on their faith. He forgave the man his sins.

We see in the act of these men an acknowledgment of who Jesus is and what such an acknowledgment means in life. Jesus verified that acknowledgment by forgiving the man's sins and healing him.

Jesus showed his spiritual power and authority by healing the paralytic. As the Son of God, Jesus had the authority to both heal the man and forgive him of his sins.

TEACHING PLANS

Teaching Plan—Varied Learning Activities

Connect with Life

1. In advance of the class meeting, find two empty two-liter cola bottles. If you can, remove the labels on the bottles. Remove the cap from one bottle, and tighten the cap securely on the other. As you begin the session, have someone squeeze the empty bottle first. The individual should be able to collapse the bottle. Then ask the same person to squeeze the bottle with the cap on it. The person may be able to make a small dent, but he or she should not be able to do anything like what happened to the first bottle. (Try this in advance to be sure you have the cap on tightly enough.)

2. Ask, *What is the difference between the two bottles?* (The class will probably say it is the restriction of airflow in the second bottle, which is true. The trapped air inside the bottle keeps the bottle from collapsing.) Say to the class, *You cannot see the air, but it provides the substance that holds the bottle shape. This experiment shows us how you cannot always see what keeps items from collapsing, but you can see the evidence of its work. Today we are talking about faith. Faith is something people cannot see, but they can see the result of it.*

LESSON 2: A Faith Worth Acting On

Guide Bible Study

3. Before class, enlist a team of members to act out the incident on Mark 2:1–5. (You might also combine this activity with the teams in step 4, thus having three teams.) Guide them to use the *Study Guide* material, including the sidebar, "Through the Roof," to develop the skit. Allow the team the freedom to have an imaginary conversation similar to what the friends and the paralyzed man may have had during the event. Let them problem-solve aloud about how they are going to get their friend before Jesus. Suggest that the paralyzed person talk about how their ideas are not going to work and how embarrassed he is going to be as he is lowered through the roof. (A copy of the instructions can be found in "Teaching Resource Items" for this study from www.baptistwaypress.org.) At the conclusion of the skit, ask, *How would you have felt helping this friend? What are some contemporary situations where helping a friend might be like this story of faith?* Help the group see that sometimes it is their faith that God uses to save or heal the person.

4. Divide the group into two teams. One team should have the focus of being a pro-Jesus team, believing Jesus could forgive sins and heal. The other team should be "teachers of the law," who questioned and opposed Jesus' authority. Refer the teams to the information in "A Healing Controversy" in the *Study Guide*. (A copy of the instructions can be found in "Teaching Resource Items" for this study from www.baptistwaypress.org.) Ask, *What have you just been a witness to? How do you think this is possible? How does this make you feel about this man Jesus?*

Encourage Application

5. Using "Implications and Actions" in the lesson in the *Study Guide*, discuss the three principles from this episode in Jesus' ministry. Ask the group how these implications and actions would play out in today's world. You also may want to ask whether members could give examples of how they have seen these principles in action.

6. State that today's lesson has brought to our minds and hearts that our faith is something worth acting on. Give each person a sheet

of paper and ask them to write this heading on it: "A Faith Worth Acting On." Ask them to turn to the person next to them and talk about opportunities they know of where an act of faith is required to make a breakthrough. After they have identified a situation, tell them to write it on the sheet of paper. Then ask them to think of a situation in their lives in which they need to act in faith and to make a covenant with their partner to "act in faith" in that situation.

7. Close with a prayer acknowledging the power of Jesus Christ to forgive sin and heal the sick. Pray that our faith would be the type of faith that makes the difference in many people's lives.

Teaching Plan—Lecture and Questions

Connect with Life

1. Ask, *How do you feel when you read or hear about a story that seems hard to believe? What causes the disbelief?* State that today we are studying an incident that if it were in the *Capernaum Times* would cause similar discussion—a paralyzed man was healed!

Guide Bible Study

2. Enlist someone to read aloud Mark 2:1–5 while the class listens for what happened. Share with the group the information in the *Study Guide* under the heading, "The Faith of Four Friends," and the small article, "Through the Roof." After the presentation of the material, ask the group to think about the passage from the viewpoint of several different people. The first view would be that of the friends. Ask, *What kind of friendship would it take to do what these friends did for the paralyzed man? How would you rate their level of determination and why?* The second viewpoint would be that of the bystander, watching the event. Ask, *Why do you think the people were doing this for the paralyzed man? What do you think about their tearing up someone's roof? What were you thinking Jesus was going to do with this man coming through the roof?* The last viewpoint is that of the paralyzed man. Ask, *How embarrassing do you think this was*

for the paralyzed man? What do you think the paralyzed man thought about what was happening? Help the group explore the various thoughts about the healing.

3. Invite someone to read aloud Mark 2:6–12 while the class listens for the viewpoint of another group. Explain the verses by using the *Study Guide* comments under the heading "A Healing Controversy." Emphasize the controversy that the "teachers of the law" had over Jesus' authority to forgive sin and heal the sick. Ask, *Why did Jesus forgive the man's sins before healing him? What would Jesus' healing the man say about Jesus' forgiving the man?*

Encourage Application

4. Write on the board these three statements from the "Implications and Actions" section of the lesson in the *Study Guide*:

   - The faith of a community has power.
   - Faith is manifested in action.
   - Jesus has authority in both the physical and spiritual realms.

   Ask the group to give practical ways they see each of these happening today. If they do not see one or more of them happening, ask them to consider ways they could happen in their community.

5. To explore the Scriptures further and see how they apply to our lives, ask the questions in the *Study Guide*. Be certain to ask question 6.

6. Close the session by asking members to think about people and situations where their faith can make a difference. Pray that God will use you and your faith to make a difference next week in someone's life.

Focal Text

Mark 2:13–17, 23—3:6

Background

Mark 2:13—3:6

Main Idea

Jesus supersedes all religious and cultural rules and traditions.

Question to Explore

To what extent are Christians unbound from religious and cultural rules, and who gets to decide?

Teaching Aim

To lead the class to determine principles and implications for life today about observing religious and cultural rules

UNIT ONE

Good News Today

Lesson Three

Live the Unbound Life

BIBLE COMMENTS

Understanding the Context

Jesus was in his ministry in Galilee, the northern section of the nation of Israel. He centered his ministry around the Sea of Galilee, which was a dominant feature of the area. Capernaum seemed to be the base of his operations.

Capernaum was a major town located on the northwest shore of the Sea of Galilee. Simon Peter and his brother Andrew as well as Matthew lived in Capernaum. Other disciples of Jesus, perhaps even James and John, apparently also lived in Capernaum. Designated a city, the implication is that it was a larger place than simply one of the fishing villages that dotted the seashore.

Probably because of its proximity to a major east-west trade route, Capernaum had a customs station located there. A military installation under the command of a centurion was also located in Capernaum. Fishing and farming were the major economic activities.

The ministry of Jesus was preaching, teaching, and healing. Although Mark's Gospel includes some of Jesus' teachings, it concentrates on the activity of Jesus. Having already called two sets of brothers—Peter and Andrew, and James and

John—Jesus gathered a group of followers. Jesus chose these men as he went about his ministry throughout the area.

Jesus' ministry in Galilee was not without its problems. The people came to hear him in droves. But the religious leaders often disputed his actions and his teaching. Mark 2:1—3:6 includes five disputes or controversies between Jesus and the Jewish religious leaders. We studied the first controversy in lesson two, and the background passage for this lesson contains the four additional controversies.

Interpreting the Scriptures

Call (2:13–14)

Jesus "once again" walked along the shore of the Sea of Galilee. A large group of people gathered around him. He began to teach them. A common practice of rabbis was to walk surrounded by a group and to teach as they walked.

During the walk they came to a tax collector's booth that a man named Levi was in charge of. We usually identify Levi with Matthew, one of the twelve disciples who followed Jesus. As Jesus did with the two sets of brothers earlier, Jesus said to Levi, "Follow me." Levi also responded immediately. Levi got up from his desk in the tax collector's booth and followed Jesus. With no questioning or hesitation, he simply followed Jesus.

Tax collectors were not popular people. Generally the government in that day farmed out the collection of taxes to local tax collectors. The tax collector owed a certain amount of money to the government. He could keep what he collected above that sum. Many tax collectors used that system as an excuse for extortion and became wealthy from it. The Scripture does not indicate whether Levi collected taxes for the Romans or for Herod Antipas, the ruler in that area. Both used the same system. Since Capernaum was located near a major road, the taxes may have been import-export taxes or simply taxes on all items passing through.

Jesus chose as one of his followers a person others would have shunned. Jesus reached out to all people. Levi responded in obedience. While the Scripture does not specifically state it, we assume that in following Jesus Levi repented of his past action, quit his position as tax collector, and acted in obedience to the call of Christ. Repentance and obedience are demanded of all who follow Jesus.

Companionship (2:15–17)

2:15–16. Jesus was at a group meal at Levi's house. Other tax collectors were present. They were probably Levi's friends since tax collectors would have had few other friends. "Sinners" were also eating with them. "Sinners" does not necessarily indicate the morals of the people. "Sinners" were people who did not pay particular attention to the Jewish law, especially as the Pharisees interpreted it. Pharisees and others who paid close attention to keeping the law in detail considered them "sinners."

Mark observed in this verse that many people who followed Jesus were also there. Also present were the "teachers of the law." The Greek text (as well as NASB and NRSV) clarifies that these "teachers of the law" were Pharisees. The Pharisees were the largest of three main Jewish parties of the first century. They were very concerned about keeping the law in detail, especially the oral interpretation of the law. Their very name indicated separatism.

Dinner parties were not necessarily private events. People often hung around and observed those who were eating together. When the Pharisees saw that Jesus ate with "many tax collectors and 'sinners,'" they were upset. They asked the followers of Jesus why he would eat with tax collectors and sinners. In an effort to keep themselves pure, the Pharisees would never have companied with such a group.

Notice that the followers of Jesus were called "disciples." A disciple is a learner, one who follows another and learns from him.

2:17. Jesus overheard the Pharisees' question to his disciples. Jesus' answer to them showed his purpose. Just as a physician does not hang around healthy people but goes to those who are sick and in need of a physician, so Jesus went to those identified as "sinners." His purpose in the world was not to call the righteous, those already in right standing with God, to repentance but those who needed repentance.

In 2:18–22 "some people" observed that the followers of John the Baptizer as well as the Pharisees fasted. The Jewish law required fasting only on the Day of Atonement (see Leviticus 16:29; 23:29; Numbers 29:7). The Pharisees fasted twice a week (Luke 18:12). The people asked why Jesus and his followers did not fast this same way. Jesus answered that his coming was a celebratory event, not a sad occasion. With his coming, new understandings of freedom called for new behavior.

Clarification (2:23–27)

2:23. On a Sabbath Jesus and his followers apparently took a short cut through a grain field. As they walked through the field, they reached down, picked a few heads of the grain, rolled them in their hands to get the husks off, and ate the grain. This was a common practice and was allowed by the Jewish law. They likely did it often, but this was on a Sabbath.

2:24. Following along with them and always on the lookout for an infraction of the law, the Pharisees both observed and commented on this activity. They pointed out that this was an infraction of the Sabbath law. The disciples were both reaping and threshing.

2:25–26. Jesus answered the Pharisees with a historical precedent. The incident is found in 1 Samuel 21:1–6. Actually Ahimelech was the priest involved. His father Abiathar was the high priest at the time. Since Abiathar was high priest, the event is referenced to his time rather than to the priest involved. David was fleeing from Saul, and he and his hungry followers ate the consecrated bread. That which was consecrated helped David and his followers.

2:27. Jesus followed that comment with a pronouncement on the purpose of the Sabbath. The Sabbath was created for humans. The Sabbath was a day of rest and worship. Human beings were not created for the good of the Sabbath but the other way around. Referring to himself again as the Son of Man, Jesus indicated that he was the Lord of the Sabbath. If the Son of Man is Lord, and thus is over all, he is over the Sabbath also. The Sabbath laws do not rule him; he rules over the Sabbath laws. Too, the Sabbath laws are to help people, not hinder them. The Sabbath was intended for the well-being of people.

Conflict (3:1–6)

3:1. On another Sabbath Jesus went to a synagogue to worship. The location of this synagogue is not noted. Another worshiper in this synagogue was a man with a "shriveled" (NIV) or "withered" (NASB, NRSV) hand. Always acting with compassion, Jesus noticed the man.

UNIT ONE: Good News Today

3:2. The Pharisees who had dogged Jesus were in that synagogue, too. Worship was not their only purpose there. They were watching Jesus carefully to see what he would do. They were looking actively for something they could use to accuse him.

3:3. What Jesus did was to order the man to stand before the congregation. He wanted everyone there to see what would take place.

3:4. This pronouncement of Jesus came in the form of a question. He asked them whether it were lawful on the Sabbath to do good or to do evil, to save a life or to take a life. The answer to the question is obvious. To do good, to save life, would always be in order. The Pharisees could not answer that question. They were "silent."

3:5. Angered by their response and distressed by their stubbornness, Jesus commanded the man to stretch out his hand. As the man stretched out the shriveled hand, he was healed. The hand could now work properly.

3:6. This miraculous healing sealed Jesus' doom. The Pharisees joined with the Herodians in plotting Jesus' death. The Herodians were the third of the major Jewish parties. While the Pharisees and the Sadducees were basically religious parties, the Herodians were secular. They were supporters of Herod, the puppet king. This was a strange coalition. Normally the Pharisees would not team with the Herodians on anything. But the conflict between Jesus and the religious leaders had deepened to the point that they determined Jesus must die.

Focusing on the Meaning

Jesus continued to gather people to him in commitment and obedience. He even called unlikely people to his service. In calling Levi, a tax collector, Jesus showed his inclusiveness. No one, even those despised and rejected by the common people, was outside Jesus' interest, concern, and care. Levi responded to Jesus in obedient commitment.

Not only did these kind of people follow Jesus, but also Jesus openly fellowshipped with them. At a meal in Levi's home, Jesus was questioned about eating with those whom others considered sinners, people who were not careful in keeping the religious traditions. Jesus responded to that criticism with the observation that physicians go to the sick, not the healthy, to give healing. Jesus came into the world to call those who needed his help and his presence.

The cultural traditions of the time did not bind Jesus. When his followers plucked a few heads of grain, rolled them in their hands, and ate them, they were accused of breaking the Sabbath law by reaping and threshing. Jesus pointed to historical precedent by David's using consecrated bread for the relief of his followers. That which was consecrated was intended to help people, not harm them.

Too, deeds of goodness could be performed on the Sabbath day. In a synagogue at an unnamed place Jesus healed the shriveled hand of another worshiper. The question then was whether the intent of the Sabbath was to do good and heal or to do harm and hurt.

These conflicts with the religious rulers sealed Jesus' doom. They could not overcome his teachings and his actions. But they would plot his death.

TEACHING PLANS

Teaching Plan—Varied Learning Activities

Connect with Life

1. Begin by asking, *Do you know how to train fleas?* Someone in your group may know the story of training fleas. If someone knows the story, invite the person to tell it. If no one knows the story, share the following information. Have a glass jar with a top on it. Set it in front of the group. Tell them this is all you need to train fleas. You simply put the fleas in the jar with the top on it, and the fleas will jump and jump, hitting their heads on the jar lid. After a week of letting the fleas hit the lid, you can take the lid off the jar and the fleas will stay in the jar. You simply have placed limits on the fleas. As a result, they have succumbed to the jar and will never leave the jar. They have lost their ability to jump out of the jar. Their behavior has been changed. (Warn the group not to try this at home until they become professionals.)

THE GOSPEL OF MARK: *Jesus' Works and Words*—Teaching Guide

2. Ask the group to consider whether they think we have used traditions and limits to keep us from living an "unbound life," as the lesson title suggests. State that today's lesson deals with how Jesus dealt with the limitations people tried to place on him.

Guide Bible Study

3. Refer to the section in the *Study Guide* with the title, "Challenging the Status Quo." Summarize that section in order to provide the setting for the Scripture passage for today. Tell the group you want them to do a brief research project on the four areas of controversy Jesus faced in the Scriptures for today. Divide the group into four smaller groups. Instruct them to use the Bible passage and the appropriate *Study Guide* section to answer the questions. They are to write their findings on the board or a large piece of paper. (A copy of the instructions can be downloaded in "Teaching Resource Items" for this study at www.baptistwaypress.org.) Here are the Scripture assignments: (1) Mark 2:13–17; (2) Mark 2:18–22; (3) Mark 2:23–28; (4) Mark 3:1–6. Here are the questions each group is to use in studying their assigned passage:

    (1) What was the controversy Jesus faced in this passage?
    (2) What were the reactions by those who questioned Jesus' actions?
    (3) What Old Testament Scripture did Jesus' questioners use to try to prove Jesus wrong?
    (4) How did Jesus react to the disapproval?
    (5) Are there traditions that keep us from serving God and ministering to people as Jesus wants us to do? If so, what are some ways we can approach these traditions in light of what Jesus did and taught?

4. After about twelve minutes, bring the groups back together to report on their findings. After each presentation, lead the whole group to comment. After all have reported, encourage the group to focus on question 5 about traditions. Then use the following case studies to lead the class to consider a modern version of a controversy similar to what Jesus faced.

- *Case 1*: A Christian sees a person who needs some counsel and encouragement, but this person is not a person of good social standing. The Christian feels a strong sense of God's leadership to help the person. How, when, and where would you approach this person to help the person?
- *Case 2*: A child in the community has received a bad report from a cancer test. Her family is told she only has six-to-nine months to live. The news comes right in the middle of Christmas preparations. Amidst all the preparations of Christmas, how would you reorder your Christmas to share the love of God with a family who needs the healing of Jesus in their lives?

Encourage Application

5. Display again the jar you used for the flea-training story. Use the *Study Guide* section "Implications and Actions" to reinforce the idea that we live an "unbound life" in Christ.

6. Give each person in the group a piece of paper and a small jar with a lid on it. On the piece of paper, write the phrase "Unbound Life." Then ask them to place it in the jar and screw the lid on it. Then tell them to put the jar where they can see it daily. Encourage them to let the jar remind them that Christ enables his followers to "live the unbound life." Encourage them to remove the jar lid when they experience a situation in which they feel Christ enables them to "live the unbound life." (You may want to encourage them to tell of this occasion next week and return the jar lid to you. If so, celebrate each jar lid that you receive back from a member.)

7. Pray that God will give each person the desire and ability to live an "unbound life."

Teaching Plan—Lecture and Questions

Connect with Life

1. Summarize the introduction material about moving and change in the *Study Guide*. Then set the scene for this Scripture passage by reviewing the *Study Guide* material on "Challenging the Status Quo."

2. Ask, *Who establishes the religious status quo for us?* Write down on a piece of paper or the board the answers to the question. (If someone answers "Jesus," God," or "the Holy Spirit," probe further by asking whether we sometimes let our culture and other people do that.)

Guide Bible Study

3. Invite someone to read aloud Mark 2:13–17. Summarize "Eating with Sinners" in the *Study Guide*. Add additional insights as seems helpful from "Bible Comments" on these verses in this *Teaching Guide*. Then ask:

   - Who are the twenty-first century tax collectors and sinners we are not to eat a meal with or otherwise associate with today?
   - Why are we not to eat with them?
   - Are there traditions we need to break to reach these people?

4. Read aloud Mark 2:18–22. Explain these verses, using the information in the *Study Guide* under "To Fast or Not to Fast." Ask:

   - What was the purpose of fasting?
   - What was the conflict Jesus had about fasting?
   - Is there anything in our world today that would be like this controversy of fasting?
   - How should we deal with the controversy in light of Jesus' teachings in this passage?

5. Enlist someone to read aloud Mark 2:23–27. Explain the incident by using the information in the *Study Guide* under the heading "Working on the Sabbath," and "Bible Comments" on these verses in this *Teaching Guide*. Ask:

- What was the controversy Jesus faced with the Pharisees concerning work on the Sabbath?
- What was Jesus' point in reminding the Pharisees about what David did?
- What was the purpose for which God intended the Sabbath to be used?
- Do any traditions limit our ministry to people today?

6. Have someone read aloud Mark 3:1–6. Explain the incident by using the information in the *Study Guide* under the heading "Healing on the Sabbath," and "Bible Comments" on these verses in this *Teaching Guide*. Ask:

    - What controversy did Jesus face with the Pharisees about healing on the Sabbath?
    - How did Jesus challenge them to change their minds?
    - Are there any traditions that limit us today in this area of ministry?

7. Refer to "Questions" in the *Study Guide*. Ask the class to think about question 1 for themselves. Then ask questions 2–5 and wait for responses for each.

Encourage Application

8. Invite comments about what the class thinks are implications of this lesson for their lives. Consider also using the case studies in step 4 in the other teaching plan.

9. Show each member of your group a twelve-inch ruler. (If you have access to free or inexpensive rulers or can make them, give each participant a ruler.) Tell them that this is an instrument to measure length according to a rigid standard. On the other side of the ruler, write the words, "God's Love." Tell them that God's rules should always be administered only with a heavy dose of God's love and grace. Challenge the members to seek opportunities in the coming week to cross traditional barriers to administer God's love.

10. Pray that God will give us wisdom to know his law and administer it in love and thus to live an "unbound life."

Focal Text
Mark 4:21–34

Background
Mark 4:1–34

Main Idea
Who Jesus is and what the results of his ministry are and will be are more, much more, than meet the eye.

Question to Explore
When worldly power and methods seem so often to be what works and prevails, does it make sense to stake our hopes and futures on Jesus and his way?

Teaching Aim
To lead the class to suggest implications of these parables for Jesus' work, their church, and their lives

UNIT TWO

Showing Who Jesus Is

Lesson Four

More Than Meets the Eye

BIBLE COMMENTS

Understanding the Context

After healing the man with the shriveled hand in an unnamed synagogue, Jesus withdrew from that place to the Sea of Galilee, continuing his Galilean ministry. So many people continued to follow him and press around him that he ordered a boat in which to leave the area (Mark 3:7–12).

Jesus chose twelve people, whom we usually label the disciples or the apostles, who would be his closest companions. These Twelve would travel with him and learn from him. A disciple is a learner, one who learns from another. Jesus would also "send them out to preach and to have authority to cast out demons" (3:13–19).

Such mighty things were done at Jesus' hand and so many people continued to crowd him everywhere he went that some, including some in his earthly family, thought he had taken leave of his senses. Others, particularly the Jewish religious leaders, accused Jesus of acting in the power of Satan. But Jesus reminded them that Satan would not use his powers to defeat himself. He warned them of the danger of attributing the work of God to the work of Satan. He also reminded them his true family was composed of those who did the will of God. This was the family to whom Jesus and all people of faith belonged (3:20—34).

The crowd following Jesus around grew so large that Jesus used a boat as a platform for speaking. Getting into the boat, Jesus pushed off from shore. With the crowd lining the seashore, Jesus taught them. Primarily he taught in parables.

The earliest definition of a parable I learned was that a parable is an earthly story with a heavenly meaning. At times, although not usually, a parable may be allegorical, which means that each element stands for something. Usually a parable has only one point, and you should not push the details in interpreting it. Some parables, however, may make more than one point in their meaning. Jesus consistently used parables in his teaching. Through the use of parables he could get his message across to those with the spiritual insight to understand it while others would not perceive what he said.

With the parable of seeds Jesus showed that the word of God would fall on some unexpected places. All who heard it would not be receptive to it. But some would. The kingdom of God, the rule of God, would ultimately blossom forth.

Mark characteristically gave more attention to the actions of Jesus than to the teachings of Jesus. He did, however, provide some of the parables of Jesus.

Interpreting the Scriptures

Illumination (4:21–25)

4:21. In verses 10–12 Jesus stated that parables could be used to obscure the truth from those who do not understand it. In this wisdom statement used as a parable in verse 21, Jesus showed that a parable can be used to reveal the truth to those who see it. Jesus stated this teaching in the form of two questions. Each would have *yes* as the answer.

A lamp in those times was a bowl filled with olive oil in which a wick was placed. The obvious purpose of a lamp was to illuminate, to give light. Since its purpose was to give light, a person would not put a lighted lamp under a bowl or under a bed. Instead, the person would place the lamp on a lampstand so it could illuminate the area around it.

4:22. Jesus answered his own questions by observing that the purpose of the lamp is to show what was hidden, to bring out into the open what had been previously concealed.

4:23. Then Jesus made the application. Anyone who has the ability to hear should hear and heed what he taught. The meaning is not that one has the physical ability to hear, but that the person heeds and applies what is heard.

4:24–25. Jesus followed that parable with a statement that is both a promise and a warning. A person should watch carefully what he or she hears and heeds. Whoever hears, understands, and accepts what Jesus taught about the rule of God in his or her life will receive even more insight. The further you go in following Christ, the more you understand about its meaning. You will have even more blessings from God. That is the promise.

The warning is that when a person does not hear with perception and thus does not act on what he or she hears from Jesus, that person will become less spiritually perceptive. If an individual does not act on what is learned, the ability to respond spiritually will be lessened. The truths and blessings of God become less meaningful to that individual. This passage is often used in teaching about stewardship, but it applies to all of the Christian life.

Intention (4:26–29)

4:26. Jesus told a parable to describe the nature of the kingdom of God. Using an agricultural metaphor, Jesus described how God intended to rule in human lives and how the kingdom of God grows.

When a farmer planted his fields, he spread the seed over the ground by broadcasting it. He walked along the field throwing out the seed by hand from a bag or basket.

4:27–28. The seed that was broadcast over the field took root, sprouted, and grew. This natural growth process took place whether the farmer was aware of it or not. As the farmer went about his normal activities whether asleep or awake, the seed sprouted and grew. The farmer did not know how this process worked; he just knew the process was occurring. The soil produced the fruit in order: first the stalk, then the head, and then the kernel in the head of grain.

4:29. When the grain was fully ripe, the farmer took his sickle and harvested it. The harvest is God-given. The growth of God's kingdom is also God-given.

God intended for his kingdom to grow in this natural way. As the seed of the word of God is planted in the lives of people, it will take root and grow. The intended harvest is fully mature believers.

Increase (4:30–32)

4:30. Jesus continued his description of the kingdom of God with another comparison from nature. This description was also introduced by two questions: What is the kingdom of God like? And, how can it be described by a parable? Teaching by parables was often introduced by a question.

4:31. Jesus again answered his own questions by using the description of a mustard seed that grows into a tree.

The mustard seed may not literally have been the smallest seed planted. But it was a very small seed and was characteristically used as a proverb for smallness. The people could relate immediately to what Jesus said.

4:32. The mustard seed was very small when it was planted. But it would grow. The mustard seed would grow into a bush or tree that could reach the height of ten or twelve feet. So what began as an extremely small seed grew to a bush or tree large enough that birds made their home in its branches.

The point of this parable is the growth of the kingdom of God from very small beginnings. The parable does not really concern what the branches and birds represent. The movement inaugurated by Jesus and his small band of followers looked small at the time but eventually would have far-reaching results.

Interpretation (4:33–34)

4:33. Mark indicated that he had not collected all the parables Jesus used in teaching. Rather the parables in this section of the Gospel were representative of the teaching of Jesus and selected to fit the purpose for Mark's Gospel.

Jesus used the parables to teach the "word" to them. "Word" refers to the word of God described in Mark 1:14 as the gospel, or the good news. This is the message that God loved us so much he became one of us. Jesus,

THE GOSPEL OF MARK: Jesus' Works and Words—Teaching Guide

the Word of God made flesh, lived a sinless life, performed mighty works, and showed the love and mercy of God. Ultimately Jesus gave himself in self-sacrifice on the cross and was resurrected from the dead. Of course, at the time the death and resurrection of Jesus would not be a part of the content even though Jesus would hint at it several times to his followers. During his lifetime they never got the hints.

Jesus taught his hearers "as much as they could understand." That statement does not mean they were dense or incapable of understanding much that Jesus said. Instead, it means Jesus did not go beyond their comprehension in teaching them. He taught them at the level at which they could grasp the meaning.

4:34. Jesus' preferred method of teaching was through parables. The meaning of the word parable is *something laid alongside* for the purposes of comparison and understanding. In teaching in parables Jesus used the common experiences of life and comparisons with nature and agriculture. These were things his listeners could understand and to which they could relate.

Jesus used the parables in teaching publicly. When he was alone with the Twelve, he would explain the meaning of the parables to them. He wanted to make sure they understood what he said.

Focusing on the Meaning

In reading the teachings of Jesus in parables we realize there is more than meets the eye. Using what were apparently simple stories and analogies, Jesus taught eternal spiritual truths. What could appear to someone as simply engaging stories were really abiding, deep, spiritual truths.

When we discover who Jesus is—the incarnate Son of God, God in human flesh living and working among us—we are not to hide this truth from the world. Just as one does not put a lamp under a basket, but instead puts it on a lampstand so that the lamp can illuminate a room, we are to display this discovery. Jesus came into the world to illuminate the dark places of the human heart, to bring light and hope where there had been only darkness and despair. This witness we give to the world.

Some things are God-given. Even as the farmer cannot understand how the seed he has sown develops into a mature crop, we do not understand how the witness of Christ will increase throughout the world. That

LESSON 4: More Than Meets the Eye

expansion and the secret of it is more than meets the eye. We are called to serve Christ faithfully, even though we do not, and can not, know the ultimate outcome.

God's rule in human life, the kingdom of God, may seem to start out small, as insignificant as a small seed. But it will grow to great size. We do not know the ultimate reach of the kingdom of God, but we do know that it has expanded greatly since its small beginning with Jesus and his followers. We know, too, that it will continue to expand even beyond our expectations. The effects of the teachings of Jesus are always more than meet the eye.

TEACHING PLANS

Teaching Plan—Varied Learning Activities

Connect with Life

1. Prior to the session, enlist someone—from another class in the church, if necessary—who can give a five-to-seven minute testimony of a time when God demonstrated his power by bringing a solution to a problem or challenge the person thought was unsolvable or impossible. Examples might include: healing from a disease; a financial burden being lifted; finding employment; being saved from a dangerous situation. If no one is available, as the class arrives, lead the class to make a listing on the board of examples they have heard about personally.

2. Invite a person to read the Main Idea for today's lesson from the *Study Guide*, "Who Jesus is and what the results of his ministry are and will be, are more, much more, than meet the eye." State, *If we can learn to apply the teachings of Jesus, the possibilities of God working in our lives are limitless. Many times what at first seems impossible from our perspective becomes possible when we look deeper into the life of Jesus and listen intently to his teaching. Today we will travel with the disciples to learn how to understand and apply some kingdom principles for our daily lives.*

The Gospel of Mark: *Jesus' Works and Words*—Teaching Guide

3. Using the information in "Understanding the Context" in this *Teaching Guide*, briefly summarize Mark 3:7—4:20. Make sure to include a definition of the term *parable*.

Guide Bible Study

4. Divide the class into two groups. Assign one group Mark 4:21–25. Assign the other group Mark 4:26–32. Instruct the first group to read the assigned Scriptures and to develop a list containing as many different purposes for which a lamp might be used as they can and also to identify what they think these verses mean. Instruct the second group to read the assigned Scriptures and to develop a list of truths related to planting and harvesting and also to identify what they think these verses mean. Refer the groups to the information in the *Study Guide* on their assigned verses.[1] After about seven minutes, call for reports. As each report is given, guide the discussion using the *Study Guide* comments and information in "Bible Comments" in this *Teaching Guide*. (A copy of the assignments can be downloaded in "Teaching Resource Items" for this study from www.baptistwaypress.org.)

5. Call for a volunteer to write on the board the following heading, "Principles to use when meeting the needs of others." Enlist someone to read Mark 4:33–34. Ask the class to identify effective methods of communication or principles of ministering to people in these two verses. If necessary, use the comments in the *Study Guide* under the heading, "The Best Way to Teach." Then, ask them to add to the list by examining Mark 4:21–32. Examples might include: telling many stories with the same meaning; using simple language; talking to both groups and individuals; explaining truths; being realistic about results; using the right method.

6. Either at this point or at the conclusion of the class session, ask the class to bow their heads for a brief prayer. Share with the class your desire for God to teach through you each week to accomplish great things for God's kingdom. Ask a volunteer to voice a prayer for you that you could apply the methods of Jesus in your teaching.

Encourage Application

7. Divide the class into pairs. Refer the class to "Questions" in the *Study Guide*. Instruct each pair to read and discuss questions 1 and 2.

8. After about five minutes, call for the class to reassemble. Give each person a small index card. Ask each person to list on the card two places where they could "scatter the seeds of God's word and trust God for the results." Examples might be work, home, family, and the like, but encourage them to get more specific. Examples might be a person's name, the break room at work, children's baseball practice on Tuesdays, etc. Refer to "Implications and Actions" in the *Study Guide*. Encourage each person to place the card in a visible spot to serve as a reminder that we are to let our light shine and to spread the seed of God's word. Close by stating, *Go and tell your Jesus story to someone who needs a message of hope, and trust God to do mighty things!*

Teaching Plan—Lecture and Questions

Connect with Life

1. Prior to class, write on the board, "When worldly power and methods seem so often to be what works and prevails, does it make sense to stake our hopes and futures on Jesus and his way?" As the class arrives, ask them to discuss this question with a partner.

2. Prior to class, obtain and bring a small lamp, a small jar of soil, and a tiny bag of very small seeds. Also, if possible, bring a piece of glass and a pair of prescription eyeglasses.

Guide Bible Study

3. Read the Main Idea of today's lesson to the class. Ask for someone to lead the class in prayer. Call for reports from the question in step 1. Then state, *Today we are going to hear three stories that will provide us with principles to live the Jesus way and encouragement to watch for the mighty movement of God in our lives.*

THE GOSPEL OF MARK: *Jesus' Works and Words*—Teaching Guide

4. Encourage the class to watch while you place the lamp on a table near the front of the room. Before class, make sure it can be plugged in and has a working bulb, but do not turn it on at this point. Using the information in the *Study Guide* and "Bible Comments" in this *Teaching Guide*, explain Mark 4:21–25. As you lecture, turn the lamp on and off several times. Make sure the lamp is off, and then ask, *Reflecting on the parable of the lamp, what are some things that threaten to darken your light?* After they have mentioned a few, read Mark 4:23. Then turn the lamp back on, and leave it on.

5. Place the jar of soil underneath the lamp. Using the information in the *Study Guide* and "Bible Comments" in this *Teaching Guide*, explain Mark 4:26–29. Have someone read out loud Mark 4:1–8. Now ask the class whether they agree with the following statement, *We must share the good news of Jesus Christ but leave the results to God.* Allow a couple of minutes for responses, but be careful not to allow more than about five minutes.

6. Open the jar, and pour the seeds into the soil. Show the class how small a seed is on your hand. Using the information in the *Study Guide* and "Bible Comments" in this *Teaching Guide*, comment on Mark 4:30–32. Then ask, *Can you think of any "mustard seed" opportunities God provided for our church in the past?* After responses, continue, *What "mustard seed" opportunities do you think God may be placing on the horizon for our church?*

Encourage Application

7. Instruct the class to locate and read the small article in the *Study Guide*, "Mustard Seeds of Yesterday." Then ask, *How do you think the work of Christ might be more than meets the eye today?* Call for examples of ministries that may seem small now, but that God might use in a big way in the future. Continue, *What other implications do you see in these parables for our church and our lives?*

8. Invite someone to turn the lights off in the classroom. Once done, the lamp that is still on will bring into focus the jar with the seeds. Read Mark 4:33–34 aloud. Ask participants to bow their heads. Say, *I encourage you to ask Jesus at this time to show you through these parables how you can be a light and scatter seeds on the soil in and around your life*

to advance God's kingdom. Allow about one minute for silence. Then close with prayer.

NOTES

1. If class attendance is larger than twelve, form additional groups using duplicate assignments in order to keep group size to no more than six participants.

Focal Text
Mark 4:35—5:43

Background
Mark 4:35—5:43

Main Idea
Jesus specializes in helping people in situations that seem hopeless.

Question to Explore
What can we do when the situation seems hopeless?

Teaching Aim
To lead the class to identify the common elements in the events of this passage and state implications for their lives of what Jesus did in each

UNIT TWO

Showing Who Jesus Is

Lesson Five

Jesus and Hopeless Situations

BIBLE COMMENTS

Understanding the Context

No hope. Hardly anything strikes as much fear in the human heart as the observation that there is no hope. Jesus met many situations in which there was apparently no hope. But in each of these seemingly hopeless situations, Jesus acted with an overarching power over the forces of nature and human disabilities.

In Mark's Gospel the section dealing with parables is followed by a section telling of miracles performed by Jesus. Four miracles of Jesus are recorded in this section. The healing miracles of Jesus were always in response to human need. Jesus refused to spin off a miracle for a miracle's sake. Jesus was still engaged in his Galilean ministry, a ministry in and around the area surrounding the Sea of Galilee.

Mark showed the nature and character of Jesus by what he did. In Mark's Gospel the actions of Jesus are very important. In this section of miracles Jesus acted in response to human need. In each case, Jesus was called upon to act, and act he did. As Jesus met with human need that ran all the way from fright due to the conditions of nature to uncontrolled forces at work in human life to debilitating physical disabilities to even death itself, he acted. Acting with compassion and power, Jesus met the needs of people with a miracle. Jesus brought hope and healing to hopeless situations.

Interpreting the Scriptures

Fright (4:35–41)

4:35–36. In Mark 4:1, Jesus got into a boat and pushed off from the shore to teach the people who were gathered on the shore of the Sea of Galilee. When evening came, Jesus instructed his disciples that they go across the lake to the other shore. He may have done this to avoid the crowds. Or he may have decided to take his ministry to the other side of the lake. Not disembarking from the boat, Jesus and his disciples headed across to the other side. Other boats followed along with them.

4:37–38. Probably exhausted from the day's activities, Jesus went to sleep on a cushion in the stern of the boat. Suddenly a squall developed on the lake, a squall so serious that the boat was almost swamped.

Squalls were common on the Sea of Galilee. The east side is mountainous with many ravines. The wind can funnel through the ravines onto the surface of the lake, churning it into a dangerous waterway quickly.

When the storm came, Jesus was so trustful of God that he slept. The disciples were fraught with fear. Waking Jesus from his sleep, they asked, "Teacher, don't you care if we drown?" Their fear expressed itself in almost a rebuke to Jesus. "Teacher" was one of the titles often used for Jesus. Jesus was recognized as an authoritative teacher.

4:39. Being awakened from his sleep, Jesus showed he did care. He commanded the wind, "Quiet! Be still!" The wind obeyed! The howling wind died down. and the lake was calm. A similar expression is used in Mark 1:25 when Jesus exorcised a demon.

Jesus showed his power even over the forces of nature. The winds and the waves obeyed his command.

4:40. The disciples had rebuked Jesus. Now he rebuked them. Contrasting fear and faith, he asked them why they had no faith. In the face of the forces of nature, they feared for their lives rather than having faith God would save them.

4:41. Now the disciples had fear of a different kind. Terrified in the presence of the power of Jesus to calm even the winds and the waves, they asked themselves who Jesus was that even the winds and the waves obeyed him.

Mark had already identified (1:1) Jesus as the *only-one-of-his-kind* Son of God. In following Jesus, the disciples had acknowledged this truth. But they did not yet understand all it meant.

Flight (5:1–20)

5:1–5. Jesus' ministry was not limited to one area. Crossing to the east shore of the Sea of Galilee, Jesus and his disciples came to an area known as "the region of the the Gerasenes" (or Gadarenes). The region took its name from a city some miles from the lake. The region was Gentile territory and was probably controlled by the named city.

Disembarking from the boat, Jesus was met by a man with an unclean or evil spirit. This crazed individual lived in the caves that were used for tombs. Banished from the society of other people, he was forced to sleep in the tombs. Of all but superhuman strength, he could not be bound by ropes or chains. Throughout the day and night he would shriek with terrifying sounds. He abused himself by cutting and bruising himself with stones, possibly trying to beat the evil spirit out of his body. This man was as storm-tossed by the demons as Jesus and his disciples had been stormed-tossed at sea.

5:6–8. Seeing Jesus, the man ran to him and knelt before him. Addressing Jesus as the "Son of the Most High God," he asked Jesus in a loud voice what Jesus wanted with him. He begged Jesus not to "torture" him. On more than one occasion the demons recognized Jesus for who he was (1:24, 34; 3:11). As they addressed Jesus as the Son of God, they recognized his power over them.

Jesus rebuked the demons as he had rebuked the sea. He commanded the evil spirits to come out of the man.

5:9–10. The ancients believed that if you knew a person's name you had some measure of control over the person. Jesus asked the name of the evil spirit. The evil spirit replied that his name was "Legion." A Roman legion was composed of about 6,000 men. It was as though 6,000 evil spirits inhabited this man.

After revealing the name to Jesus, once more the evil spirit requested that Jesus not send them out of the area. Demons were often thought to inhabit a particular area.

5:11–13. Demons were also thought to have to occupy something. Nearby was a large herd of pigs. Negotiating with Jesus, the demons asked Jesus to send them into the pigs. Jesus agreed to that. The evil spirits left the man and went to the pigs. The herd of pigs, numbering about 2,000, then rushed over the steep bank into the sea and were drowned.

5:14–15. Those who had tended the pigs ran immediately throughout the area telling what had happened to their pigs. Hearing that kind of news, many people from the area rushed to the site.

When they arrived they found an amazing sight. The demonic man, whom people must have known well, was found calmly sitting there. He was fully clothed—and more amazing—he was in his "right mind"!

5:16–17. This result caused fear among the people. Upon hearing the story, they were so afraid, in fact, that they asked Jesus to leave the area. If Jesus had that kind of power, what else might he do?

5:18–19. Jesus acceded to their request. As Jesus got into the boat to leave, the man whom he had healed asked to go along with him. Jesus denied that request. Instead, he gave an assignment to the man.

Jesus told the man to go home and tell the people who knew him what Jesus had done for him. To those who had known him as demented and uncontrollable, the man was to tell how much the Lord had done for him and how much mercy the Lord had showed him. He would be restored to his family. Notice that Jesus attributed the miracle to the "Lord" but Mark identified the miracle with Jesus. Where Jesus acts, God acts.

5:20. The Decapolis was an area of ten basically Gentile cities on the east shore of the Sea of Galilee. The demented man made sane went throughout the area giving witness to what God had done for him through Jesus Christ.

Fatigue (5:21–34)

5:21–24. Going back to Galilee, Jesus was once again met by large crowds of people. Among those in the crowd was Jairus, a synagogue ruler. Likely he was an administrator in the synagogue.

Jairus had an urgent request for Jesus. Jairus's daughter was dying, and he asked Jesus to come and lay hands on her to heal her. Whatever else Jairus may have known about Jesus, he must have known of his healing of the sick in Galilee. He expressed faith that Jesus could heal her and that she would live. Jesus agreed to go with him. A crowd pressed around him.

5:25–29. In the crowd was a woman who had been hemorrhaging for a dozen years. She had tried all sorts of remedies. In fact, she had exhausted her resources on physicians. Instead of improving, her condition had worsened. Because of her condition she was ritually unclean.

The totally fatigued woman had heard about Jesus. She thought that if she could move quietly behind him and just touch his garments he had such power that he would heal her. That she did. Upon touching Jesus' garment, the woman realized her bleeding had stopped immediately.

5:30–31. Jesus asked who touched him. He realized his healing power had been manifest. The disciples incredulously asked how he could ask that question. People were crowded all around him.

5:32–34. Jesus kept looking for who had touched him Approaching him with fear, the woman admitted she was the one. She told him her story. Jesus assured her that her faith had brought about her healing. He assured her she would be free from that disability, and he urged her to go with peace in her heart.

Futility (5:35–43)

5:35–36. While Jesus was still speaking with the woman, servants of Jairus arrived to say it was futile for Jesus to come. The girl was dead. Jairus had no need to bother Jesus any more.

Jesus ignored their report. He told Jairus to believe and not to be afraid. Once more Jesus contrasted fear with faith.

5:37–39. Taking only Peter, James, and John with him, Jesus went to Jairus's house. Seeing all the weeping and wailing over the girl's death, Jesus asked why all the commotion. He asserted that the girl was not dead, but rather she was only sleeping. The people laughed at that; they knew death when they saw it.

5:41–43. Dismissing everyone but the parents and the disciples he brought with him, Jesus went to the child. Taking the twelve-year-old girl by the hand, he commanded her to get up.

Immediately she not only got up but also walked around. To show she was really alive, Jesus ordered food for her to eat. He warned the people not to spread the word that he had power even over death, the final foe.

Focusing on the Meaning

Jesus showed he had power over the elements that frighten and disable people. Storms, dementia, disability, disease, and even death are subject to Jesus' power.

Jesus made no distinction between those who benefited from his ministry. Prominent people like Jairus as well as unnamed people like the suffering woman are alike objects of God's grace through the power of Jesus. Status is of no matter to Jesus. Human need does matter to him.

Neither is Jesus' power limited to certain areas. People in Galilee and in the Gentile territories alike knew of God's grace through Jesus' acts.

When people find themselves in situations that are considered hopeless, Jesus acts to give healing, wholeness, health, and deliverance. Before Christ, no situation is truly hopeless.

TEACHING PLANS

Teaching Plan—Varied Learning Activities

Connect with Life

1. Bring several current magazines and newspapers to the class along with scissors and appropriate tape for use on the wall or a poster board. On a sheet of poster board, write "Storms in Life?" Tape this item to the middle of a focal wall. Do not use the markerboard area. (If you prefer not to use this activity involving magazines and newspapers, you could just ask people to name the difficult and seemingly

hopeless situations in the news in the preceding week. Substitute this approach for steps 1 and 2.)

2. As people arrive, instruct them to work in small groups or individually. Ask them to search through the magazines and papers to locate any pictures, words, or headlines that represent situations that seem hopeless. Tell them to cut or tear them out and, using the tape, attach them to spots on the poster on the focal wall. Allow about ten minutes for this activity. (Examples might include deaths, car accidents, stress, financial issues, divorce, crime, and similar situations.)

3. Spend a few minutes highlighting or reading the examples on the poster. Then, enlist someone to read the Main Idea of today's lesson from the *Study Guide*, "Jesus specializes in helping people in situations that seem hopeless." Invite someone to pray, asking the Holy Spirit to have control as the lesson is taught today.

Guide Bible Study

4. Divide the class into three groups of six or fewer people each. Assign each group one of the following Scripture passages:

   - Mark 4:35–41
   - Mark 5:1–20
   - Mark 5: 21–43

   Instruct each group to read the story and answer these two questions: *What was the primary crisis they were facing? What did the individuals in each story do when their situation seemed hopeless?* (A copy of the assignments can be downloaded in "Teaching Resource Items" for this study from www.baptistwaypress.org.)

5. Write the following title on the markerboard: "Storms in Life." After about seven minutes, call for reports from each group. As the reports are given, enlist a volunteer to write key words from each report under the heading on the board. (Examples might include dangerous situations, illness, demon possession, death, lack of faith, prayer, talk to Jesus, beg, and plead.)

6. Ask the following questions and allow time for answers:

   - Why do you think Jesus went to sleep when he perhaps knew a storm was coming up?
   - In your opinion, why did Jesus allow the demons to go into the pigs?
   - Why do you think the woman touched the robe of Jesus instead of talking to him?
   - In your opinion, why did Jesus evidently allow the girl to die rather than healing her at long distance?

   Remember these are opinions. The idea is to encourage participants to think about the Scriptures they just read and to consider the opinions of others in the class rather than to arrive at "right" answers. Be careful on time when leading this discussion. You may not be able to ask all the questions. Allow at least ten minutes for the steps in "Encourage Application."

Encourage Application

7. Ask participants to think once again about the items they placed on the poster (or named) at the beginning of the session. Distribute a small index card to each person. Give these instructions: *Define a current storm you are facing by jotting down words or two or three sentences about it on the card.* Assure them they will not need to share these with the class. Then after a couple of minutes, tell them to write their fears related to this storm on the back of the card.

8. Ask each person to focus on what they have written as you read Psalm 23. Then tell them to write on the side of the card with the storm definition the word "HOPE" in large letters on top of that definition. Instruct them to turn the card over as you read Colossians 1:27, emphasizing the words, "Christ in you, the hope of glory." Then ask them to write in large letters across their fears, "JESUS."

9. Close the session by encouraging participants to claim for themselves the hope Jesus offers and to "go and tell others" about the hope in Christ as the demon-possessed person did.

The Gospel of Mark: *Jesus' Works and Words*—Teaching Guide

Teaching Plan—Lecture and Questions

Connect with Life

1. Prior to class, write on the board, "Fear or Faith." If possible, locate the hymn "The Solid Rock"[1] to use later in class.

2. Distribute a piece of paper and a pen or pencil to each person in the class. Ask them to write the words "Fear or Faith" at the top of the piece of paper. Explain that they will use this today to identify examples of fear and faith during the class session.

3. Refer to the Main Idea of today's lesson in the *Study Guide*, and read it to the class, "Jesus specializes in helping people in situations that seem helpless." Enlist someone to read aloud the small article in the *Study Guide* labeled, "All People Count." Then voice a prayer for the class.

Guide Bible Study

4. Using the *Study Guide* comments and "Bible Comments" in this *Teaching Guide*, present a brief lecture on Mark 4:35–41. Remind the class to write on their paper examples of fear and faith they may notice as you speak. Then ask, *Why do you think Jesus went to sleep when he knew a storm was coming up?* Allow a few minutes for the class to discuss. Read Psalm 62:5–6 to the class, and ask someone to pray a brief prayer thanking God for protection from life's storms.

5. Invite someone to read aloud Mark 5:1–20 while the class listens for what happened. Using the *Study Guide* comments and "Bible Comments" in this *Teaching Guide*, explain these verses. Remind the class about continuing to make their lists (see step 2). Then ask, *Why do you think Jesus sent the demons into the pigs?* Allow time for discussion. Read Romans 12:12, and call for someone to pray a brief prayer thanking God for his mercy.

6. Have someone read aloud Mark 5:21–43 while the class listens for the two incidents that occurred. Using the *Study Guide* comments and "Bible Comments" in this *Teaching Guide*, present a brief lecture on Mark 5:21–43. Explain to the class that this will be their last

Lesson 5: Jesus and Hopeless Situations

chance to add to their continuing list of fear and faith examples. Then ask, *Why do you think the woman touched Jesus rather than talk to him?* After a few answers, ask *Why do you think Jesus evidently allowed the girl to die rather than just healing her at long distance?* After a time of discussion, call for someone to pray a brief prayer thanking God for his healing power.

7. Ask, *What do you think are some of the common elements in all of the incidents in the passage of Scripture for today?* Follow up by asking, *What are some implications for our lives of what Jesus did in each of them?*

Encourage Application

8. Lead the class to mention a few of the fear and faith examples they wrote down on their paper. As they do, summarize and write them on the board under the title, "Fears or Faith." Remind the class of these biblical truths:

   - God protects us *in* the storm but not always *from* the storm.
   - God often brings healing and help not only for the benefit of the individual but also to provide a means to share his grace with others.
   - All types of people in all types of circumstances are valuable to God.
   - Every blessing and every miracle generates new responsibilities.

9. If you located the hymn, "The Solid Rock" (see step 1), read one or two stanzas and the chorus to the class. Then, ask the class to identify one person they know who needs hope. Encourage them to write that name at the bottom of the paper they have used to take notes. Then, challenge them to write down one action to help that person. Finally, close with prayer asking God to provide a time to do what they have just listed.

NOTES

1. Words, Edward Mote; music, William B. Bradbury. See *The Baptist Hymnal* (Nashville, Tennessee: Convention Press, 1991), no. 406.

Unit Two: Showing Who Jesus Is

Focal Text

Mark 7:1–23

Background

Mark 7:1–23

Main Idea

True goodness—and evil—come from within and not from keeping the norms of tradition and culture, even Christian tradition and culture.

Question to Explore

How can we keep faith from hardening into mere tradition?

Teaching Aim

To lead the class to contrast the approach of Jesus and the Pharisees and to identify implications for being people of genuine faith

UNIT TWO

Showing Who Jesus Is

Lesson Six

When Cleanliness Is Not Next to Godliness

BIBLE COMMENTS

Understanding the Context

Continuing his ministry in Galilee, Jesus "went to his hometown," Nazareth (Mark 6:1). As he customarily did, given the custom of allowing visiting rabbis to teach, Jesus taught in the Nazarene synagogue on the Sabbath. Those who heard Jesus teach "were amazed" (6:2).

They may have been amazed, but many of them were not impressed. They could think of nothing but Jesus' background. They recalled Jesus' family. They remembered his work as a carpenter. In fact, they were offended at his teaching. The result was such an atmosphere of unbelief and rejection that Jesus could perform no major miracle at Nazareth. A few sick people were healed. But it was as though the power of God was stymied by their rejection and unbelief (6:2b–6).

Moving from village to village, Jesus extended his ministry by commissioning the twelve disciples to go in pairs throughout the area. He empowered them to minister in his name and through his power. As they ministered, they saw many amazing results (6:7–13).

John the Baptizer was imprisoned and then executed by Herod, the puppet king. Herod was puzzled at the teaching and the popularity of Jesus. He wondered whether perhaps Jesus was even the man whom he had executed now risen from the dead (6:14–29). Others, too, no doubt, wondered about the identity of Jesus.

But they continued to seek Jesus. As he sought a quiet place to be alone with his disciples, Jesus was confronted with a great crowd of people. Late in the day after teaching the people, he asked for them to be fed. They, too, must be exhausted and hungry. The disciples protested that there were no resources to buy the amount of food needed. Jesus asked what they had. They turned up five loaves and two fish. A little in the hand of Jesus can be much. He had the people sit in groups. The five loaves and two fish proved sufficient to feed—and even to have leftovers—5,000 men, not counting the women and children (6:30–44).

Jesus sent the disciples ahead of him in a boat across the Sea of Galilee. He stayed behind to pray. Seeing that the disciples were having trouble because the wind was against them, he walked to them across the water. They were terrified at the sight of him. They had already forgotten, or not applied, the experience of the feeding of the 5,000. Jesus again contrasted faith and fear. He then got into the boat with them and once more calmed the sea (6:45–52).

They landed at Gennesaret on the northwest corner of the Sea of Galilee. The people recognized Jesus and brought sick people to him by whatever means they could. Jesus healed them. Even those who merely touched his clothes were healed (6:53–56).

Interpreting the Scriptures

Event (7:1–5)

7:1. Even though Jesus was ministering in Galilee, a group of people from Jerusalem in the south came to observe him. The impression is that this group had come from Jerusalem to inspect the activities of Jesus. They gathered around Jesus as he taught.

The Pharisees were one of the major parties of the Jews. They were dedicated to keeping the law. Their name means *the separated ones*. To understand the law better, they had developed oral traditions about the meaning of the Jewish law as well as the written tradition. Actually, as far as being determined to keep the Jewish law scrupulously, the Pharisees were the best first-century Judaism could offer. They carried the attempts to keep the law of God to an extreme.

They were joined with the "teachers of the law "(NIV), called "scribes" in other translations (NASB, NRSV). These people not only copied the law, but they also interpreted the law. They were the authoritative interpreters of the meaning of the Jewish law.

7:2. As the Pharisees and scribes observed Jesus, they noticed that some of his followers were eating food with hands that were unclean. This did not mean their hands were caked with dirt and grime but rather that their hands had not been ritually washed. The "unclean" or "unwashed" hands were contrasted with holy or consecrated hands.

7:3–4. Mark explained that the Pharisees and all the other Jews who were serious about scrupulously keeping the law had a ritual, ceremonial way to wash their hands. The disciples, though, had not washed their hands in the proper elaborate ritual manner. The prescribed manner of washing the hands had become an established tradition, "the tradition of the elders."

The Gospel writer further explained that whenever these people would come from the marketplace, they would wash their hands in this ceremonial way. The concept was that uncleanness could be passed on. If their hands touched something in the market that was ritually unclean, they could contaminate other things they touched.

The ceremonial cleansing did not stop with the hands but extended even to the kitchenware and utensils: "cups, pitchers and kettles." The Pharisees and scribes were extremely careful to keep the traditions. They did not want anything to be defiled ritually.

7:5. With this background, you can better understand the question of the religious leaders on the inspection team. They wanted to know why Jesus' disciples did not follow those religious traditions rather than eating with hands that were not ritually clean.

Evasion (7:6–13)

7:6–7. The first part of Jesus' answer to his critics was a quotation from Isaiah 29:13. The point of the quotation is that to them ritual purity was more important than piety. They might give lip service to God, but they did not follow God in obedience. Their worship of God was empty because they followed human rather than divine instruction.

LESSON 6: When Cleanliness Is Not Next to Godliness

In doing that, they were "hypocrites." A hypocrite was one who played a role. The word has to do with pretense and insincerity. In this case, they were not so much concerned with the ritual purity of Jesus' followers as in catching them in an infraction of the Jewish law as they interpreted it.

7:8. Jesus completed that statement by charging that they had forsaken the commandments of God for the instructions of their human teachers.

7:9. In the second part of the answer of Jesus to the religious leaders, he illustrated how they had substituted human teaching for divine commandments. He observed that they had perfected a method for getting around the Lord's teachings.

7:10–12. Citing Exodus 20:12 and 21:17, Jesus showed how the religious leaders maneuvered their religious beliefs to keep from caring for their aging parents properly. The law specified their responsibility in caring for their parents in their declining years. They escaped that responsibility by declaring the resources they could use to care for them to be "Corban." Mark also offered a word of explanation for "Corban." Something that was "Corban" was a gift dedicated to the service of God.

When a person declared that what he had was dedicated to God, "Corban," then he did not have to use those resources for the parents' care. The implication is strong that the Pharisees and scribes used all of it in that way. Thus, they were left with nothing to use for the parents' support. Too, they may have just made the pronouncement about the money. They may not actually have used it as a gift dedicated to God.

7:13. By this action the Pharisees and scribes had nullified God's commandment. Jesus indicated that the higher commandment was to honor their parents. By elevating the secondary to a primary position, they had annulled God's purpose. Too, Jesus indicated that was not all they had done. What he had cited was but one illustration of their putting their own traditions above the law and purpose of God.

Enunciation (7:14–15)

7:14. In the third stage of Jesus' answer to the religious leaders, "Jesus called the crowd to him" and enunciated an important principle. He called on all those present to both hear and understand the principle.

7:15. The principle is that a person is not defiled by what goes into his body. None of the food a person might eat would make him defiled or "unclean."

What really defiles a person is what comes out of the body. Jesus was not referring to human waste matter in this statement. Rather, what issues from a person from the standpoint of actions and attitudes is what Jesus had in mind.

Explanation (7:16–23)

7:16. Verse 16 is not found in most of the modern translations of the New Testament because it was not found in some of the earliest and best manuscripts of the Gospel of Mark.

7:17. After the crowd dispersed and the disciples were in a house together with Jesus, they asked him the meaning of the parable recorded in 7:15.

7:18–19. Acting almost irritated at them, Jesus asked whether they were so dull in understanding that they could not see the truth in what he said. Jesus asserted that nothing that enters a person from outside the body can actually defile that person, or make the person "unclean." Food does not go into a person's heart. "Heart" refers to the center of emotion and will in the human life, not the internal organ.

Food ingested into the body goes through the normal digestive process. The food is eaten and digested, and some of it is eliminated as waste. Understanding this natural process means that all food is therefore cleansed. The Jews considered some foods clean and others unclean. Jesus was stating that the food they ate was not unclean simply because the hands were not ritually washed. Due to the natural digestive process, all food is ultimately "clean."

7:20. What makes a person unclean is what comes out of that individual, not what goes in. Jesus was stating the importance of moral cleanliness as opposed to ritual cleanliness.

7:21–22. Jesus then gave a list of vices. These acts and attitudes come from within an individual. These are the kind of things that really defile a person.

These acts harm others. They begin with "evil thoughts." This is followed by six acts that are in the plural in the Greek: "sexual immorality, theft, murder, adultery, greed, malice." Jesus then added six characteristics in the singular: "deceit, lewdness, envy, slander, arrogance and folly."

7:23. All of these acts come from within a person. These are the things that make a person "unclean" or defiled. Ritual has little to do with it; moral uprightness does.

Focusing on the Meaning

Our extended family was at Toledo Bend Reservoir in Louisiana. My wife called to come to lunch. In the lunch call, she also told her nephew who was six or eight at the time to wash his hands. He said, "Why? I haven't touched anything dead."

"Cleanliness is next to godliness" we have always been taught. But the cleanliness emphasized by the Pharisees and scribes focused on particular types of cleanliness that, according to their thinking, could separate one from God rather than bring one to God.

Traditions are very strong. But some of our practices and traditions can reflect more of our human desire for order than of our spiritual search for Christlikeness. Keeping the tradition rather than following the leadership of the Holy Spirit may assume importance for us. When was the last time your church changed the order of service, for instance?

The religious leaders of Jesus' time were more interested in getting the ritual right than they were in moral cleanliness. Jesus emphasized moral cleanliness. He showed what really defiled an individual.

Moral cleanliness comes from within. That is more important than what goes into the body from without. Our lives are to reflect what is in our hearts—faith in Christ.

TEACHING PLANS

Teaching Plan—Varied Learning Activities

Connect with Life

1. Prior to class, enlist a student who is comfortable at reading dramatically in front of the class and who can speak clearly and strongly. Instruct the reader to be prepared to read Mark 7:1–23. If the person wishes, he or she can even come in first-century costume. If someone cannot be found, consider a tape, CD, or video that might contain these verses.

2. Write on a markerboard the following three words: "Tradition," "Legalism," and "Hypocrisy." Leave space for additional words under each heading or beside each word. As the people arrive, give each person a sheet of paper.

3. Invite everyone to consider those words as they listen to the reading of Mark 7:1–23. Ask the reader to read Mark 7:1–23 to the class. After the reading, ask each person to write a simple definition of each of the following words in their own words on one side of the paper: "Tradition," "Legalism," and "Hypocrisy." Explain that there is no one answer you are looking for and that all answers are needed.

Guide Bible Study

4. Call for several volunteers to read one of their definitions to one or two of the words. Make sure at least two possible definitions are read for each word. Use as many different people as possible. Affirm each response as you write some of the key words or phrases on the markerboard under each heading.

5. After several minutes, invite someone to read the Main Idea of today's lesson, "True goodness—and evil—come from within and not from keeping the norms of tradition and culture, even Christian tradition and culture." Explain to the class that today's lesson will

help us gain a better understanding of how to be a person of genuine faith.

6. Encourage the class to locate in the *Study Guide* the small article, "Who Were These Guys?" Enlist three different people to read one of the definitions found in this article. Ask, *Do you think people who fit into any of these categories exist today in our churches?* Suggest that all three types exist even today in all churches even if those official titles are not used. Emphasize that just like today, in biblical times not all in these categories were necessarily bad people.

7. Divide the class into two or three groups if possible. Instruct them to turn their piece of paper over and write the three words "Tradition," "Legalism," and "Hypocrisy" across the top of the page, forming three columns. Give the following assignment to each group: *Read Mark 7:1–23 and make a list of examples, words, phrases, or ideas related to these three words from the text.* (A copy of the assignment can be found in "Teaching Resource Items" for this study from www.baptistwaypress.org.) Allow about ten to twelve minutes for this activity. Then call for responses from the groups. Be aware there may not be enough time for all groups to share every one of the responses they listed. It might be best to allow each group to share only one at a time to ensure some responses from each group are heard.

8. Read Jeremiah 17:9 to the class. Then ask, *How do you think this verse might relate to the Scriptures we studied this morning?* Allow a few minutes for responses. Then read Mark 7:20–23 while the class listens for what really makes a person "unclean."

Encourage Application

9. Ask the class the following questions and encourage them to write their response on the piece of paper. Assure them their answers will not be shared with the class.

    - Identify a tradition in your life that you need to make sure you do not place above genuine faith.
    - Identify a part of your life that you tend to be a bit legalistic in when practicing it.

The Gospel of Mark: *Jesus' Works and Words*—Teaching Guide

- Identify an area in your life where at times you may be hypocritical.

10. Ask the class to bow their heads and close their eyes. Remind them that actions come from attitudes in our hearts. Encourage them to ask Jesus to change them inside. Challenge them to give their responses from step 9 to Jesus and to ask the Holy Spirit to empower them to be a person of genuine faith. Allow about one minute of silence and then close in prayer.

Teaching Plan—Lecture and Questions

Connect with Life

1. Prior to class write the following question on the board, "In what ways does our society emphasize the importance of appearance?"

2. Also prior to class, purchase a large candy bar. Gently open one end and remove the candy. Replace the candy bar with something like sand, mulch, or sticks. Gently close the end again with tape or glue. This will be used later in the session.

3. As the class arrives, ask them to discuss with a partner the question on the board. After a few minutes, ask for responses. Then read the Main Idea of today's lesson. Lead the class in prayer.

Guide Bible Study

4. Read Mark 7:1–23 to the class while the class listens for the various groups that appear in the passage. Then ask them to locate in the *Study Guide* the small article, "Who Were These Guys?" Ask them to read along silently as you read the article. Using the *Study Guide* comments, summarize the last lesson or two in order to put today's lesson in context (see also "Understanding the Context" in this *Teaching Guide*). Then challenge each person to determine which of the three—Pharisees, scribes, or elders—they can identify with the most as you present the lesson.

Lesson 6: When Cleanliness Is Not Next to Godliness

5. Using the comments from the *Study Guide* and "Bible Comments" in this *Teaching Guide*, present a brief lecture on Mark 7:1–4. Emphasize that the disciples were not in violation of the Scriptures, only tradition. Ask, *What traditions, good or bad, does our church cherish?* After several responses, remind the class that traditions are not necessarily bad unless they are placed above Scripture.

6. Using the comments from the *Study Guide* and "Bible Comments" in this *Teaching Guide*, present a brief lecture on Mark 7:5–19. Organize the material as follows:

    - Jesus' response to the Pharisees and teachers of the law (Mark 7:5–13)
    - Jesus' response to the crowd (7:14–15)
    - Jesus' response to the disciples (7:17–19)

    Ask, *Why do you think the disciples, who were closest to Jesus, did not understand these teachings much if any better than did the Pharisees or the crowd?*

7. Using the comments from the *Study Guide* and "Bible Comments" in this *Teaching Guide*, present a brief lecture on Mark 7:20–23. Explain the definitions of each of the evil intentions. State, *Jesus repeated the message about true cleansing and genuine faith five times in this passage.* Now refer the class to Mark 7:15, 19, 20, 21, and 23, reading each verse slowly. Ask, *What are some ways in Christian society or church that we tend to emphasize the outward appearance of spiritual truths?* Examples might include stained glass, the cross, and other religious symbols. Remind the class that in and of themselves, nothing is wrong with these items unless we substitute the symbol for the truth behind it.

Encourage Application

8. Invite the class to bow their heads and close their eyes. Ask them to respond silently as you read the questions in the small article, "Bringing It Home," in the *Study Guide*. Then ask them to open their eyes.

9. Now, show the class the candy bar. Read to them the name of the candy bar and the slogan or descriptions that may be written on the packaging as well. Ask for a show of hands, *Who would like to take this*

home with you? Then smile and say, *Be careful. It's what's inside that counts.* Open the bar and pour out the "trash" inside. Close by leading the class in prayer, asking God to transform the "trash" in our hearts to a treasure he can use to help us become people of genuine faith.

LESSON 6: When Cleanliness Is Not Next to Godliness

Focal Text
Mark 8:11–26

Background
Mark 8:1–26

Main Idea
We must open our eyes and overcome our blind spots if we are to see Jesus clearly and respond accordingly.

Question to Explore
What would we be able to see and understand about Jesus, about ourselves, and about other people if we would open our eyes and overcome our blind spots?

Teaching Aim
To lead the class to analyze the blindness of the Pharisees, the disciples, and the blind man and to identify implications for our seeing who Jesus is more clearly

UNIT TWO

Showing Who Jesus Is

Lesson Seven

There Are None So Blind

BIBLE COMMENTS

Understanding the Context

Jesus moved from Galilee northeast to the city of Tyre. Tyre was located on the coast of the Mediterranean Sea in the area of Phoenicia, which was a part of Syria. He entered a house, perhaps for a time of rest or a time to teach the disciples. But Jesus' presence could not be kept secret. A woman who was Greek but was a native of that area sought him out. She requested healing for her daughter, who had an evil spirit.

In another of his enigmatic statements, much like a riddle, Jesus told her he had come to minister to his people, the Jews. Jews often called the Gentiles "dogs." With a witty, insightful reply, she indicated that even the dogs could eat the crumbs that fell off a table during the meal. Jesus assured her that her daughter was healed. No one was excluded from the compassionate ministry of Jesus, even Gentile women. Jesus went beyond the prejudice of the Jews (Mark 7:24–30).

Jesus continued his journey from Tyre to Sidon farther north on the coast. Then he looped back to an area southeast of the Sea of Galilee known as Decapolis because of a group of ten Greek cities located there. In that area a deaf and mute man was brought to him for healing. Upon healing the man, Jesus asked the people not to tell it. But, of course, they did talk about it. The people were amazed that Jesus could heal even a person who was a deaf mute. Jesus probably gave the command not to tell because he did not want to be known simply as a sensationalist. The people observed that Jesus did all things well (7:30–37).

During that period of time another large crowd gathered around Jesus. Jesus recognized they had been with him for three days and had not eaten. He was afraid they would collapse from hunger as they went home if he sent them away. Summoning his disciples, Jesus asked how much food they had. They were able to come up with seven loaves of bread and a few fish. With that food Jesus fed 4,000 men as well as women and children. They even had leftovers. Then Jesus again crossed the Sea of Galilee (8:1–10).

Interpreting the Scriptures

Sign (8:11–13)

8:11. Mark does not give the origin of this delegation of Pharisees. Possibly they too had journeyed from Jerusalem to inspect Jesus as in 7:1. That they questioned Jesus indicates they did not come for just a friendly visit. They came to probe, to inquire, and to question what he did, why he did it, and by what power he did it.

They even devised a test for Jesus. Obviously, they were trying to set Jesus up. They demanded a sign from heaven to vindicate that Jesus was truly sent from God. "Heaven" is used to avoid using the name of God. What they demanded was a sign from God himself. They were not asking simply for a miracle. Miracles they had already seen. They were asking for a heavenly manifestation of some sort. They demanded divine proof.

8:12. Exasperated at their request, Jesus "sighed deeply." Then he asked why they continually needed a sign. They could have observed all Jesus had done and received all the confirmation they needed. But they wanted a specific sign done at a specific time for proof. He had already provided many signs if they would just recognize them.

Consistently refusing to perform a miracle for a miracle's sake, Jesus refused them. He stated that no sign would be given them. The miracles of Jesus were always for a purpose. Through them he relieved human need and revealed God. Jesus would not perform a miracle just to satisfy an investigative committee. He had just fed 4,000 men with seven loaves of bread and a few fish. Why couldn't they accept that?

8:13. At that, Jesus left them. He refused to be pushed into proving his divine power and authority. Getting into the boat, he crossed over to the other side of the Sea of Galilee. Jesus must have been displeased with the attitude of the Pharisees and their continual questioning of his activities.

Sufficiency (8:14–21)

8:14. Perhaps hungry, the disciples realized they had only one loaf of bread in the boat. As Jesus had apparently embarked hurriedly on this trip, leaving the Pharisees who had questioned him, the disciples had not made provision for meals.

8:15. Since they were concerned about bread, Jesus warned them to watch out for the yeast or leaven of the Pharisees and of Herod.

Yeast was used to make bread rise. Often in that day yeast was a symbol of corruption and the spreading power of evil. The yeast of the Pharisees would be their unbelief and their continued requests for a sign from heaven to validate Jesus' acts and teachings. The yeast of Herod could refer to his adultery, murder, and ambition. Both the Pharisees and Herod would indicate rejection of Jesus and unbelief. Jesus was warning the disciples to beware of such things.

8:16. The disciples did not catch the drift of Jesus' statement. Discussing it among themselves, they decided Jesus said what he did because they did not have the bread for lunch.

8:17. Overhearing their discussion, Jesus asked them three questions. He asked why they were still talking about bread. Jesus had gone beyond mere physical bread in his statement, but they were still hung up on their own predicament of having no bread for lunch. The second question centered on their understanding. Did they still not see what he was saying or understand what he meant? The third question focused on whether their hearts were so hardened they did not have the spiritual insight to understand Jesus.

8:18–20. Jesus followed those questions with three more questions. Although the disciples had eyes to see and ears to hear, they were not using them to comprehend the meaning of Jesus' actions. Then Jesus specifically asked them about the two feeding miracles, even the number of basketfuls of leftovers they had gathered. They answered correctly.

8:21. Jesus' final question centered on the disciples' understanding. Even though they had experienced these events, they did not understand how they pointed to his identity as the Messiah. They were blind to what Jesus was doing.

Sight (8:22–26)

8:22. As Jesus landed at Bethsaida some people brought a blind man to Jesus. Asking Jesus to touch the man, they wanted Jesus to heal him. Apparently Jesus' usual method in healing blindness was to touch the eyes of the blind person.

8:23. Instead, Jesus led the man outside the village. For this healing, Jesus wanted privacy. Jesus "spit on the man's eyes and put his hands on him." Probably Jesus spit on his hands and applied the spittle to the man's eyes.

Jesus asked the blind man whether he saw anything. The account does not indicate whether the man had ever seen. He may not have been born blind but may have lost his eyesight at some time. Jesus expected him to be able to describe what he saw. Also, in 8:25 the Scripture reads, "his sight was restored." He evidently had sight at one time.

8:24. The man replied that he could see people. But he could not see them clearly. He could not distinguish any characteristics of the people. They looked to him like trees walking around, images that moved.

8:25. So Jesus once more put his hands on the man's eyes. Three verbs describe the restoration of the man's sight: "his eyes were opened, his sight was restored, and he saw everything."

8:26. As he had done with the demon-possessed man (5:19), Jesus sent the man home. He instructed him not to go into the village. Probably Jesus gave this instruction so the man would not tell anyone what had happened to him. Jesus did not need the unnecessary publicity as he made his way to Jerusalem. He also did not want to be known simply as a healer and a wonder-worker.

This healing is the only account in the Gospels in which two attempts were required for Jesus to effect a healing. This does not mean Jesus was ineffectual the first time. The difference was in the disciples and their ability to comprehend and not in the inability of Jesus to heal in the first effort. The healing is an enacted parable. Just prior to the healing, Jesus talked to the disciples about their dullness, their slowness in recognizing who he was. A second touch from Jesus would be necessary for the disciples to have their spiritually blind eyes opened.

So the passage has a symbolic as well as a literal meaning. The literal meaning is that the man was healed of his blindness. Jesus accomplished what the people who brought the man to him wanted. He healed the man. On the symbolic front, the disciples needed a second touch from Jesus before they could recognize who and what he was. Even though they had traveled with him, listened to his teachings, and seen his actions, including the two recent feeding miracles, they still had not clearly seen who he was—the Christ, the Son of God.

The next event in the Gospel account is Peter's confession of faith in Christ (8:27–30). Peter confessed that Jesus was the Christ, the Son of God. But that conclusion was rather slow in coming. Peter and the other disciples needed a second touch before they could come to that conclusion and make that confession. They, too, did not see clearly who Jesus was. Jesus had already commented on their dullness and their lack of comprehension. More than one effort, more than one experience, more than one proof was needed before they could with confidence make the confession. Then Jesus would continue to clarify the meaning for them.

Focusing on the Meaning

Some people are physically blind. They do not see. Jesus healed people who were physically blind by restoring their sight. But some people are spiritually blind. They cannot see the spiritual truths about God and Christ around them. An encounter with Jesus heals that blindness also.

Some of the spiritually blind are blind to the salvation Jesus offers. They do not believe in Jesus as personal Savior. By meeting Jesus and entrusting their lives to him in faith, they can be healed of that blindness and brought into a saving relationship with Jesus, the Christ.

Other people are blind to the spiritual truths around them. They may have trusted Christ as Savior but do not see the way this faith can be put into action in life every day. A fresh encounter with Jesus heals that blindness also.

Jesus Christ provides sufficiency for all the needs of our lives. The disciples had to be reminded that since Jesus had fed multitudes, surely he could provide for their lunch needs. So we must be reminded of how Christ has sufficiently provided for our needs again and again. He will continue to do that.

There are none so blind as those who have eyes to see—both physically and spiritually—but do not use those eyes. Jesus continually helps to open blind eyes that we may see him, God, and God's work in our midst.

TEACHING PLANS

Teaching Plan—Varied Learning Activities

Connect with Life

1. Prior to class locate and bring to the class several items associated with sight, such as a microscope, telescope, binoculars, magnifying glass, eyeglasses, and a contact lens. If you can not locate all of these, at least find two or three that serve different functions. Place these items on a table or chair at the front of the room.

2. Prior to class, write on the markerboard, "I once was blind, but now I see!"

3. As the class arrives, ask them to form at least two groups of six or fewer people each. Challenge them to discuss the functions of the objects on the table as they relate to seeing clearly certain objects. Instruct them to also identify elements or obstacles that would cause each object not to function properly. Allow about ten minutes for this exercise.

Guide Bible Study

4. Enlist a volunteer to read Mark 8:11–26 while the class listens for how the incidents relate to seeing. Then call for reports from the

exercise in step 3. Allow for as many responses as possible. Call for a volunteer to write these responses in two columns. One column will be for the *functions* while the other column will be for the *obstacles*. (Examples under the functions might include to enlarge an object, to see small parts of an object, to see objects the human eye cannot see, to bring objects that are far off closer, etc. Examples for the *obstacles* might include dirt, broken lens, wrong strength, operator error, etc.)

5. Invite a volunteer to read the Main Idea of today's lesson, "We must open our eyes and overcome our blind spots if we are to see Jesus clearly and respond accordingly." To set the scene for the focal passage, explain Mark 8:1–10 briefly by using the information in the *Study Guide* and "Bible Comments" in this *Teaching Guide*.

6. Divide the class into two groups. Form additional groups and give duplicate assignments in order to have six or fewer people in each group. Give each group the following instructions: (1) Discover possible reasons for spiritual blindness in the assigned passage. (2) Discuss how Mark 8:1–10 and Mark 8:22–26 might relate to the assigned passage. Allow about ten to fifteen minutes for this activity. (A copy of the instructions can be found in "Teaching Resource Items" for this study from www.baptistwaypress.org.) Encourage one person to give a brief report from each group's work.

   - Assignment One. Mark 8:11–13
   - Assignment Two. Mark 8:14–21

7. Invite each group to report their opinions. As each group shares, add comments as needed based on the information in the *Study Guide* and "Bible Comments" in this *Teaching Guide*. Remind the class that just as human blindness has many forms, so does spiritual blindness. (Examples might include: wrong perspective, sin, lack of faith, hard heart, etc.)

Encourage Application

8. Draw the attention of the class back to the focal board. Read the list under "Obstacles" again. Now ask the class, *What are some obstacles in our spiritual life that might relate to these words?* (Examples might include unconfessed sin, lack of relationship with Jesus, not reading

The Gospel of Mark: *Jesus' Works and Words*—Teaching Guide

the Bible or praying, ignorance, stubbornness, lack of vision, etc.) If you prefer, use instead or in addition the questions and activities under the small article, "Bringing It Home," in the *Study Guide* either with the class as a whole or in small groups.

9. Ask everyone to bow their heads and close their eyes. Then, turn the lights out. Ask the people to open their eyes as you continue to stand by the light switch. After just a few seconds, read John 8:12. Tell the class, *As you leave today, commit to letting the light of Jesus remove obstacles in your life that might cause spiritual blindness.*

Teaching Plan—Lecture and Questions

Connect with Life

1. Prior to class, write on the board or a poster the Main Idea of today's lesson, "We must open our eyes and overcome our blind spots if we are to see Jesus clearly and respond accordingly." Then use some small pieces of poster board to cover the words "open," "overcome," "blind," "clearly," and "respond."

2. Read Mark 8:1–10, indicating that this is background for today's Scripture passage. Lead in prayer or call on someone to do so.

Guide Bible Study

3. Ask, *What are some instruments we use to help us see clearly in today's world?* (Examples might include eyeglasses, binoculars, contact lenses, etc.) Read Mark 8:11–13 while the class listens for how these verses might relate to blindness and sight. Call for responses. Using the comments in the *Study Guide* and "Bible Comments" in this *Teaching Guide*, explain the verses briefly. Emphasize the statement, "When we are driven by signs, we always need more." Explain how we must be open to looking through the eyes of Jesus. Uncover the word, "open." Invite a volunteer to lead a prayer for the class, asking Jesus to open our eyes to the lesson's truth today.

Lesson 7: There Are None So Blind

4. Call for someone to read Mark 8:14–21 aloud while the class listens for what the verses suggest or state about seeing. Using the information in the *Study Guide* and "Bible Comments" in this *Teaching Guide*, present a brief lecture on Mark 8:14–21. Explain the yeast of the Pharisees and Herod. Ask them for modern examples for such yeast. Also be sure to ask question 2 in the *Study Guide*, "After witnessing the feeding of the four thousand, why did the disciples lack understanding of who Jesus was?" Emphasize that the disciples in today's focal passage were preoccupied with earthly matters, like bread, and how this kept them from seeing spiritual matters. Uncover the words "overcome" and "blind." Ask the class to mention "earthly matters" that at times keep us preoccupied.

5. Read Mark 8:22–26 while the class listens for what seems unusual in this passage. Using the information in the *Study Guide* and "Bible Comments" in this *Teaching Guide*, present a brief lecture on Mark 8:22–26. Ask the class to locate and read the small article in the *Study Guide*, "One Healing, Two Steps." Then call for comments, questions, or additions related to this article. Allow about five minutes for these responses. Then, uncover the word "clearly." Call for a volunteer to pray for the class and ask the Holy Spirit to enlighten the word "clearly" to the class today.

Encourage Application

6. Ask, *Which of Jesus' dialogues can you identify with most—the one with the Pharisees, with the disciples, or with the blind man?* Ask responders to explain why.

7. Ask question 4 in the *Study Guide*, "What steps can you take to see Jesus more clearly?" Then uncover the word "respond" on the board. Explain to the class that the only way to know whether we are seeing Jesus clearly is to act on his commands. Instruct the class to locate and read the small article in the *Study Guide*, "Bringing it Home." Invite comments. Then challenge each person to think of one action they could do this week based on today's lesson. Close with a prayer asking God to give the class the courage and strength to follow through with their commitment.

Focal Text
Mark 8:27–38

Background
Mark 8:27–38

Main Idea
The only proper place for a person to be is behind Jesus, following him, even though the way may not be easy.

Question to Explore
Where are you in relation to Jesus—ahead, behind, a long way away?

Teaching Aim
To lead the class to state the meaning of this passage for their lives and to respond to Jesus by affirming or re-affirming their commitment to him

UNIT THREE

With Jesus on the Way to the Cross

Lesson Eight

Not an Easy Way

BIBLE COMMENTS

Understanding the Context

More and more Baptists are choosing to observe Lent, the forty-day period prior to Easter. Some consider the season a spiritual pilgrimage during which they engage in self-examination and repentance. This spiritual journey ends with the celebration of Easter.

One reason Mark wrote his Gospel was to emphasize that Jesus expected his disciples to walk as he walked. Retracing Christ's journey to Jerusalem (Mark 8:27—10:52) offers excellent spiritual guidance for disciples during a Lenten journey. Jesus provided extensive training regarding discipleship as he journeyed. Themes in this section include the need for the Messiah to suffer, the failure of the disciples to grasp this, and their persistent concern with prominence in Christ's kingdom.

Mark 11:1—16:8 narrates Jesus' last days in Jerusalem. He continued to stress that disciples would find true greatness in suffering and through serving others. That he endured suffering and death affirm his conviction that he saw himself as both the Son of God and the suffering servant Messiah.

Mark 8:27–30 forms the theological center of Mark's Gospel. Mark's focus changed as he introduced Jesus' intention to journey to Jerusalem for the final days of his ministry. Jesus would spend less time with the crowds and devote more attention to training the Twelve. Luke marked this shift by stating that Jesus "determined to go to Jerusalem" (Luke 9:51).[1] Mark introduced the change with Peter's confession at Caesarea Philippi.

Previous passages in Mark have introduced Jesus as "Christ, the Son of God" (Mark 1:1). Mark has highlighted both Jesus' identity and authority as God's Son. However, Jesus attempted to silence anyone who sought to make his identity public. Reading the early chapters in Mark may have left us wondering why the disciples and crowds did not recognize Jesus as the Messiah. Only when we reach Jesus' crucifixion does a person, and a Gentile at that, state that Jesus is the Son of God (15:39). Previous statements that Jesus is God's Son were made by Mark (1:1) and unclean spirits (3:11; 5:7), and the high priest alluded to Jesus' identity as he questioned Jesus (14:61). One reason Jesus suppressed his identity was because the people had a different concept of the Messiah than he did.

Mark wanted his readers to grasp the connection between suffering and discipleship. These words are all but synonyms in this Gospel.

Mark offered two literary hints to demonstrate the connection. One was Peter's declaration that Jesus is the Christ and the apostles' subsequent misunderstanding of what being Messiah implied. The second clue is less obvious. Mark 8:22—10:52 opens and closes with Jesus healing blind men. These *bookends* may be Mark's figurative way of illustrating how the disciples had been spiritually blind, but their eyes now were being opened (see lesson seven).

Interpreting the Scriptures

Who Is Jesus (8:27–30)?

The future of Jesus' work depended on the disciples recognizing he was the Messiah. They also had to know what being the Messiah meant for both Jesus and them. Jesus took them to a location near Caesarea Philippi where he could begin to clarify this for them.

Jesus asked the disciples two questions: "Who do people say that I am?" and "Who do you say that I am?" Peter's answer indicated they recognized that he was the Christ. Their future comments indicated they did not know what being the Messiah meant.

UNIT THREE: With Jesus on the Way to the Cross

The Gospel of Mark: Jesus' Works and Words—Teaching Guide

8:27. Jesus had left Galilee, the territory ruled by Herod, to spend time alone with his disciples without interruption from the crowds. During this time, Jesus fed 5,000, walked on water, healed a demon-possessed girl, and fed 4,000. Herod had noticed Jesus and was puzzled by this miracle-worker (6:14–16). The crowds also had speculated about Jesus' identity.

Retreating to Caesarea Philippi served several purposes. It allowed Jesus freedom to visit with the disciples without feeling threatened by Herod. Caesarea Philippi was located about twenty miles north of the Sea of Galilee at the southwest foot of Mount Hermon. Located nearby was a cave and spring where the nature god, Pan, was worshiped. Mark may have considered this fact important because his original readers would have been pressured by the Roman government in its pagan worship to confess that Caesar was Lord.

8:28. The disciples' answers to Jesus' first question corresponded to Herod's guesses: John the Baptist, Elijah, or one of the prophets (6:14). Both John and Elijah were linked with divine power and were considered messengers who would precede the Messiah's coming. Jesus did not pose this question simply to gather information. His follow-up question showed that he was exploring their understanding of his identity.

8:29. Jesus pointedly asked his disciples who they thought he was. We might translate "you," as *as for you*, to capture Jesus' emphasis. Their having a proper understanding of his identity was critical for Jesus' work to succeed.

Peter answered for the Twelve ("them," 8:30). They had truly recognized Jesus as "Christ." I prefer the term *Messiah* here instead of "Christ." Both words mean *the anointed one*, but we use "Christ" so much that we often fail to grasp it is a title and not a proper name.

God had promised to send a Messiah who would trace his ancestry back to King David. He would usher in an ideal kingdom under God's rule. Most people of that day believed the Messianic deliverer would be a warrior king. He would free Israel from foreign control and restore the nation's greatness.

8:30. Peter's confession was the first time in Mark's Gospel that Jesus' disciples had stated his identity. But did they truly understand what being Messiah implied? Jesus immediately and sternly ordered them to keep this to themselves. He did not want the public to identify him as the Messiah because of mistaken ideas about how the Messiah would restore God's rule.

What Does Being Messiah Mean (8:31–33)?

Now that the disciples had identified Jesus as the Messiah, Jesus began to correct their misunderstanding of his role. That would prove exceedingly difficult, for lesson number one was that the Messiah would suffer.

8:31. Jesus chose not to apply the title Messiah to himself even after Peter used it. Instead, Jesus used his favorite self-designation, "Son of Man." Jesus could define this term as he desired because no one else used it for him. Daniel had used "Son of Man" for a heavenly figure and judge who would, at the end time, bring the kingdom to the oppressed on earth (Daniel 7:13–14). Jesus taught that the Son of Man had authority (Mark 2:10, 28); would suffer, die, and rise again (8:31, 9:31; 10:33); and would return in glory as judge and ruler (8:38; 13:26; 14:62).

The term "suffer" often means *to die on the cross.* Here we take it in a broader sense, which includes *being taunted, humiliated, and scourged.*

The Jewish religious authorities would take the initiative in tormenting Jesus. "Elders" designates lay members of the Sanhedrin. They were wealthy landholders who were highly respected by the community. The term "chief priests" includes the man who was currently high priest, others who had served as high priest, and members of the families from whom high priests were selected. "Scribes" denotes the professional teachers and interpreters of the law.

8:32–33. Jesus prohibited the disciples from telling others he was the Messiah, but he was willing to speak publicly about his suffering. Peter quickly interrupted, rejecting any notion of Jesus as a suffering Messiah. The Apostle could not allow Jesus to go uncorrected and "began to rebuke" him. This term was used earlier in Mark's Gospel when Jesus "rebuked" unclean spirits (1:25; 3:12) and ordered the wind and waves to be still (4:39). The harshness of the term accents the intensity with which Peter corrected Jesus.

Jesus spun around and rebuked Peter. "Rebuke" is the same term used in the previous verse and also suggests superiority and authority. Peter may have been implying that his understanding of Messiah was correct and that Jesus ought to listen to and learn from him. But Jesus had other ideas. He was Master and Teacher. The disciples needed to remember they were followers.

The harshness of Jesus' response to Peter is revealed in the words, "Get behind me, Satan!" Satan's tempting Jesus to compromise with the ways of the world in other Gospels (Matthew 4:8–10; Luke 4:5–8) reappears in a different context here. Peter was speaking the words of Satan and not the words of God. Jesus emphatically resisted following the world's concept of the Messiah.

Jesus' response also reminded Peter of a disciple's proper place. Peter's rebuke of Jesus may have indicated he had tried to displace Jesus as teacher at that moment. Jesus' hard words reminded Peter and the others that their proper role was following and not leading.

What Does Being a Disciple Mean (8:34–38)?

Being a disciple means following the way of Jesus, the way of suffering and self-denial.

8:34. Jesus now addressed both the crowds ("He summoned the crowd") and the disciples with additional comments about the meaning of discipleship. Jesus placed obligations on any individual ("anyone") who was considering following him.

Followers of Jesus must "deny" themselves if they expect to be disciples. This is a tough qualification. Disciples do not merely give up a specific thing or some things. They abandon themselves fully to Jesus. They renounce a self-centeredness that places self above Christ.

Followers of Jesus must "take up" their cross. This does not mean bearing burdens of sickness, financial struggles, or even caring for family members who cannot care for themselves. The message was clear in Jesus' time and in the time when Mark wrote. To take up one's cross meant to carry the crossbeam on which one would be crucified. One must make an absolute commitment to Christ to be a disciple. Half-hearted followers need not apply.

Followers of Jesus must "follow Me [Jesus]." To follow Jesus means self-denial and absolute commitment to Jesus and Jesus' way, that is, the way of the cross. Disciples assume the position of followers, looking to the leader for direction.

8:35–37. Jesus' demands are hard, but the reason for them is clear. Those who seek to find life in any way other than in Christ only lose it.

On the other hand, those who yield their lives to Jesus and the spread of the gospel (the good news of Jesus) find it. These verses may point to a future life. While that is certainly true, we need to recognize that disciples find life here on earth as well. To choose this world's ways and gain everything it offers and forfeit what life is truly about is to miss out on authentic life. The only way to obtain life is to give away one's life to Christ. Jesus used the term "soul" to mean *all that a person is*.

8:38. Faithfulness to Christ in this world affects Christ's response to us in a future existence. The negative phrasing may prevent us from seeing the statement's true force. I believe Jesus assumed his followers would be faithful, and he would never be ashamed of them. These words would have offered strong encouragement to the initial hearers of Mark's Gospel who were facing persecution and martyrdom.

Focusing on the Meaning

Every one of us must answer the question Jesus posed to the apostles: "Who do you say that I am?" Before your final answer, consider the implications, and examine the whole picture. To confess that Jesus is God's anointed, the Messiah, may not seem difficult. But knowing Jesus as the Christ and what that entails as we follow Jesus is the most momentous decision a person can make. Keep these truths in mind as you decide.

Disciples must get more than Jesus' title right. They must understand what that title implies for Jesus and for them. Affirming Jesus as Messiah is only the first step of discipleship.

Christ's way leads to a cross. Jesus knew why he had come. The Son of God came to proclaim the kingdom of God and to redeem humanity (Mark 10:45). The Son of Man must suffer to accomplish his purpose and God's will. Jesus knows the path we take to resurrection life. He knows where our journey leads. He has walked the way before us.

When we confess that Jesus is the Christ, we yield to his will. Disciples are followers. Jesus is God's Son, God's anointed. He is our Lord. Following Jesus is not a way to escape trouble. It often brings more struggles. Count the cost before accepting Jesus' invitation to follow as a disciple.

Following Jesus obligates us to deny ourselves and take up our own cross. We face the temptation to seek worldly security rather than risk our lives for Christ. We face the temptation to seek an easy way rather than accept

Jesus' rigorous demands. We want choices, not moral imperatives. We want to pick and choose what is agreeable to us, not what Christ demands of us. The way is not easy, but it is the path to life.

TEACHING PLANS

Teaching Plan—Varied Learning Activities

Connect with Life

1. Enlist two volunteers. Blindfold one. First, put the blindfolded person in front of the other and instruct them both to walk around the room. Next, put the blindfolded person behind the other and repeat. Finally, put the blindfolded person right next to the leader and repeat again. Thank the volunteers, and ask, *Which was the most difficult for the blindfolded person—walking ahead, behind, or beside the leader? Which was the easiest?*

2. State that today's lesson teaches how we must walk with Jesus—not ahead or far behind—for him to lead us.

Guide Bible Study

3. Using information in "Understanding the Context" in this *Teaching Guide*, explain the setting of this passage in the Gospel of Mark. Explain, too, that it immediately follows two amazing miracles, the *second* feeding of a huge crowd (Mark 8:1–10), and the two-step healing of a blind man (8:22–26). Then describe the geographical setting of this Bible passage using information on Mark 8:27 in "Bible Comments" in this *Teaching Guide*. After this, have someone read Mark 8:27–30 while the class listens for the questions and answers in the passage. Ask, *If you were to walk the streets of a major city and ask people at random who Jesus is, what answers would you expect?* Jot answers on a markerboard. Compare the answers to those given by the disciples in Mark 8:28. Note Peter's answer in verse 29.

Lesson 8: Not an Easy Way

Hand out pencils and paper to each person. Instruct them to answer the question, "Who do you say Jesus is?" in their own words.

4. Invite someone to read Mark 8:31–33 while the class listens for what Jesus said and how Peter responded. Ask, *Why do you think Peter rebuked Jesus? How would you explain the "things of men" versus "the things of God"* (NIV)?

    Read Mark 8:34–37. Divide into three small groups (six or fewer people in each group). Assign verse 34 to group one, verse 35 to group two, and verses 36–37 to group three. Instruct each group to rephrase the verse(s) in their own words and give an example or illustration that makes it clearer. (A copy of the instructions can be found in "Teaching Resource Items" for this study from www.baptistwaypress.org.) Call for reports from each group. Ask, *Do you think the disciples were expecting Jesus' call for self-sacrifice when they realized he was the Messiah? Why or why not?*

    Read Mark 8:34–37 again. Ask, *How is each of these precepts radically different from a materialistic, non-godly worldview—such as we often see today?*

5. Tell the class to pretend they are all going to climb Mount Everest together and have to choose a leader. Say that three or four candidates have excellent experience with extreme mountain-climbing. Ask, *What are some other characteristics we would demand from the person we choose?* Write the answers on the markerboard. Be sure that dependability and being able to trust the person are among the answers. Review the answers, drawing attention to the importance of personal faith and trust in a leader. Ask, *How would the disciples' belief that Jesus was God's Messiah affect their trust in him?* Then inquire, *How does your understanding of who Jesus is affect your willingness to trust him?* Allow a few moments for silent answers.

6. Read Mark 8:38. Ask, *Why would the disciples be "ashamed" of Jesus? How would you define "ashamed"?* Note that the *Study Guide* explains "ashamed of Jesus' words" as "to not believe them or accept them." Ask, *Would you agree that even the first step of discipleship, believing Jesus' words, can be a difficult and dangerous task? Why?*

UNIT THREE: With Jesus on the Way to the Cross

THE GOSPEL OF MARK: *Jesus' Works and Words*—Teaching Guide

Encourage Application

7. Recall the opening exercise with the blindfolded person and the leader. Say, *Let's look at that exercise as an illustration of different ways to relate to Jesus. What would be a "blindfold" for us? What are some ways we (a) get ahead of Jesus and (b) fall behind Jesus?* Encourage the class to answer each question in a creative, thoughtful fashion.

8. In advance, draw a cross on a piece of paper and make enough photocopies for each class member. (You could also cut out the crosses with scissors.) Distribute a cross to each person, and instruct each person to write on it one or more of their personal challenges to "take up . . . the cross." End with prayer, thanking Jesus that he is worthy of our trust as we carry our personal cross of following and serving him.

   Close with prayer of thanks for the privilege of following Jesus, and ask for courage to represent him boldly in our world.

Teaching Plan—Lecture and Questions

Connect with Life

1. In advance, enlist a volunteer who has special expertise and training in a particular job. This could be almost anyone: a master plumber, a construction foreman, a doctor, a lawyer, a teacher, and so on. Either through a role play with two other volunteers, or in response to your questions, interview the "expert" about how he or she would explain the process of acquiring the expertise or job function (for example, how you prepare to be a doctor) to (1) a seven-year-old child and (2) to a young adult. Stress that the description of how to gain expertise is more detailed and complicated for the older person.

2. Say, *As the disciples developed in their understanding of Jesus' identity, he revealed increasing challenges in what would be required to follow him. All disciples must understand that there is no easy way in following Jesus, and following him requires intense commitment.*

Guide Bible Study

3. Using a map plus information from "Bible Comments" on Mark 8:27 in this *Teaching Guide*, describe the location of Caesarea Philippi. Note that it was a center for several pagan religions, including Baal worship, Greek polytheism, and Roman emperor worship. Also note that Jesus was quizzing the disciples about various beliefs among the people concerning himself. Read Mark 8:27–30. Ask, *What are the differences between the answers in verse 28 and Peter's answer of "the Christ" in verse 29? What does "the Christ" mean?* Ask, *Why do you think Jesus told the disciples not to tell anyone about him?*

4. Ask, *Do you think at this point the disciples had a full understanding of what would happen to them and to Jesus? What do you think they imagined?* Call for several answers. Read Mark 8:31–37. Say, *Were Jesus' words what the disciples expected? How can you tell?* Ask, *What do you think were the "things of men" that Peter had in mind for Jesus?* Call for two volunteers to read Mark 9:30–32 and 10:32–34. Ask, *Why do you think Mark quoted Jesus repeating this prediction three times?*

5. Read Mark 8:37. Lead a discussion on the challenge of identifying with Christ, using questions such as these:

    - Why might someone be "ashamed" or "embarrassed" about Jesus and his teaching?
    - What are some ways we sometimes reveal we are ashamed or embarrassed about following Christ?
    - How can we become less ashamed and more bold as we represent Jesus Christ in our world?

Encourage Application

6. Say, *We generally think of "taking up our cross" as figurative, but it was literal for Jesus.* Ask, *What are some examples of people "taking up their cross"?* Accept several answers.

7. Refer the class to the small article, "Applying Jesus' Teachings," in the *Study Guide*. Encourage the class to make private notes and lists as suggested in the article. Challenge the class to review their notes

and follow through on any new or renewed commitments they make. Encourage any who have not placed their trust in Christ to do so.

NOTES

1. Unless otherwise indicated, all Scripture quotations in lessons 8–13 and the Christmas lesson are from the New American Standard Bible.

Focal Text

Mark 9:30–37

Background

Mark 9:1–50

Main Idea

The attitude of *me first* must be changed radically if we are to be faithful in following Jesus.

Question to Explore

So what's the problem with *me first*? Isn't that the way the world works?

Teaching Aim

To lead the class to identify ways to put into practice Jesus' call for a radical change in the idea of *me first*

UNIT THREE

With Jesus on the Way to the Cross

Lesson Nine

Me First

BIBLE COMMENTS

Understanding the Context

Jesus and his disciples had left the region of Caesarea Philippi after Peter had confessed that Jesus was the Messiah. As they traveled through Galilee toward Jerusalem, Jesus continued to teach them that the Christ would suffer and die.

As in previous sections of Mark, Jesus' actions illustrated his teachings. Mark had prefaced Jesus' first prediction of his passion (Mark 8:31) with an account of Jesus healing a blind man because he likely wanted the reader to associate the man's physical blindness with the disciples' spiritual blindness (8:22–26; see lesson seven). The intervening events between the first and second mention of Jesus' passion suggest that the disciples were increasing in understanding but had not yet grasped Jesus' teaching fully.

After Peter, James, and John witnessed Jesus' transfiguration, Peter wanted to build tabernacles on the mountain where they could remain and worship. God's voice reminded them they should listen to what Jesus was teaching them (9:1–8). Jesus was setting the agenda, not them. As they descended from the mountain, the three disciples continued to discuss what they had seen and what it meant for Jesus to rise from the dead (9:9–13).

A crowd met Jesus at the foot of the mountain. The disciples had been unable to heal a boy with a spirit that rendered him mute. The father begged Jesus to heal his son, if Jesus could. Jesus answered that all things were possible to the person who believed. Maybe Jesus was thinking of the lack of understanding of his disciples when he made that statement. The man replied that he believed, but he also prayed that if his belief were lacking, Christ would give him sufficient trust. Jesus healed the boy and affirmed the man's faith. In a private conversation with the Twelve, Jesus pointed out that their lack of faith could be increased only by prayer.

The disciples did not yet fully comprehend Jesus' teaching, and so he repeated his earlier statement. He would be betrayed, killed, and would rise again (see 8:31–32; 9:31). He would repeat the prediction a third time in Mark 10:32–34. The Twelve could not yet move beyond the deeply-rooted notion that the Messiah would set up an earthly and political kingdom (see Acts 1:6).

Interpreting the Scriptures

Travel (9:30)

Jesus was not taking a leisurely trip. He was focused on his destiny and on training his followers in what being his disciples meant for them. The time was growing shorter and the distance to Jerusalem less. The instruction was growing more intense.

"From there they went out and began to go through Galilee," states Mark 9:30. The mention of "Capernaum" (9:33) indicates that Jesus and his disciples had not left the Galilean region. Jesus was popular in Galilee. He performed many powerful miracles there. The bulk of his teaching occurred in this area near the Sea of Galilee. But the time for public teaching had passed. Jesus was now entering the final stages of his life. His work would be completed in Jerusalem, the center of Judaism and the headquarters of those who opposed him.

Jesus still sought to keep his whereabouts secret as he shifted his attention from the crowds to the Twelve. He spent more and more time alone with them, training and preparing them for the time when they would bear the burden of carrying out his work. They would herald "the gospel of Jesus Christ, the Son of God" (1:1). The phrase, "He did not want anyone to know about it," parallels the thought of Mark 8:30. He was not yet willing to declare publicly that he was the Messiah.

Prediction (9:31)

The differences between this prediction of Jesus' death and the first (8:31) are subtle but significant. This reference adds more detail to the previous teaching. Yet, this prediction does not provide some of the details the other two provide (10:33–34). The groups who would be responsible for Jesus' death are not named here and neither is the suffering described in as much detail as it will be in the third statement.

The role of human agents can be seen in these descriptions of the events. Even so, the descriptions also indicate that Jesus was not a weak and powerless victim of their conspiracies. What happened to Jesus was clearly part of a divine plan.

The word "delivered" can be translated *handed over* or *given over*. Jewish writers used the term to express martyrdom, and the early church drew on this meaning. The idea of martyrdom was important because what happened to Jesus was central to God's plans to redeem sinners. The passive verb suggests that God planned for Jesus to be handed over. The leaders could not have taken and killed him unless God had allowed it. Jesus' suffering was so certain that he spoke of it in advance as though it were an accomplished fact.

Several other differences can be noted between this and the other predictions of Christ's passion. The statement "delivered into the hands of men" denotes a broader involvement of humanity than either of the other two. All people, not just Jewish leaders and Roman authorities, were indicted. We see a second contrast between Jesus and the people through the use of "Son of Man" and "hands of men."

One common theme continued throughout the predictions. Resurrection would always follow Jesus' suffering and death.

Misunderstanding (9:32)

The disciples still failed to comprehend all Jesus was teaching them. The form of both verbs, "did not understand" and "were afraid to ask," suggests that the disciples were locked into their misunderstanding. Despite Jesus' focused instruction, they could not overcome their inability to comprehend the certainty of his death. They would finally understand it after the crucifixion and resurrection.

The word "statement" could refer back to the statement about suffering or the statement about Jesus' rising again. Likely, their misunderstanding refers to all the events associated with his passion and resurrection.

This verse also suggests they could not muster the courage to ask Jesus to explain his teachings further. Two reasons may explain their reluctance. The most obvious is they feared the same kind of rebuke Peter received at the time of the first prediction (8:33). Another reason for their hesitancy might have been they were gaining insight, albeit slowly, into what discipleship meant. They may have feared the destiny that awaited Christ and that also awaited them.

Teachings on Discipleship (9:33–37)

9:33–34. Jesus followed each prediction concerning his passion with instruction on what discipleship entailed. He and the disciples had stopped in Capernaum, maybe spending the night at Simon and Andrew's house (1:29). Jesus asked them in this private setting what they were talking about as they traveled. I suspect he asked for two reasons. First, he may have overheard only part of the conversation as they traveled in scattered groups of two and three. Perhaps he wanted them to fill in the gaps he had missed as he walked ahead of them. Second, he may have raised the question to force them to admit they were arguing about who would be greatest in the kingdom. Forcing them to divulge their thoughts and feelings offered him yet another opportunity to teach the meaning of true greatness. He would need to repeat the teaching at least one other time (10:42–45).

The word "discussing" suggests the disciples were speaking in hushed tones so no one could overhear them. They were "discussing" who was greatest among them. Because no disciple was named as the culprit, all of them likely had a *me-first* attitude. Could Peter, James, and John have thought themselves greater because Jesus had taken them with him when he was transfigured?

Although Jesus' question shamed them into silence, his intent was to teach. Mark used a threefold formula to denote that this was a formal teaching time. (1) "Sitting down" was the custom of a teacher. (2) He "called the twelve," which suggests he was directing his teaching to the inner band of disciples, those who would become the leaders of the movement after

Christ's death. (3) He "said to them" signifies that the main pronouncement of the teaching followed.

9:35. Jesus did not criticize the disciples' desire for greatness but instead redefined it in terms of servanthood and not power or prestige. The one who wants to be "first," that is, *great*, is the one who seeks to serve others rather than to be chief over them. The term "first" was used of rank and meant what was most important. Jesus was reversing the world's values, turning them upside-down.

The instruction on servanthood furthers Jesus' instruction beyond that of the first passion prediction. Jesus foresaw his glory in sacrifice and the cross.

9:36–37. This acted parable illustrates Jesus' teaching on greatness. We need to understand how the world viewed children in that day to grasp the shock value of Jesus' words. Children had no status and no rights. They were powerless. Children were utterly dependent on adults for their very existence.

Jesus elsewhere used children to illustrate the importance of being childlike in character (10:13–16). In that context, Jesus implored disciples to become like children in spirit. Here, however, the emphasis is not on becoming like a child but on how we accept children.

Imagine this scenario. A child runs by Jesus. He reaches out, draws the child to him ("taking him in His arms"), and renews his conversation with the disciples. Welcoming a child such as the one Jesus held in his arms was the same as welcoming Jesus (see also Matthew 25:31–46). *To receive* includes these meanings: *to be concerned about, to care for*, and *to show kindness to*. To welcome one "in My [Jesus'] name" was to act in the way Jesus would act, or to act in a certain way because of one's relationship to Jesus. To receive one in this manner was not only to receive Jesus but the Father who had sent him.

Focusing on the Meaning

Jesus' disciples can experience greatness through suffering servanthood. Discipleship and suffering are so intertwined they cannot be separated. Citizens of earthly kingdoms serve themselves while citizens of Christ's kingdom serve others.

UNIT THREE: With Jesus on the Way to the Cross

The *me-first* attitude Jesus encountered in the disciples' lives threatens every one of us. Overcoming a *me-first* attitude requires a radical change only Christ can accomplish. The words *me* and *mine* are ingrained in us from, dare I say, birth. While this seems to be a natural stage in child development, could it be that the people interacting with the child model the *me-first* kind of behavior and help to implant it inappropriately?

One measure of how healthy our churches are is how we treat our children. We might add senior adults to that list. Overcoming our *me-first* attitude means accepting the most vulnerable and unappreciated in our world, beginning with the people on whom we have influence personally.

All people are implicated in Jesus' suffering and death. A *me-first* attitude was at the core of the actions of those who killed him then and those whose actions still crucify him. Let us never forget our need for individual redemption.

Beware, the world kills those with an *other-first* mind-set. Society crucified the one who pointed out sin. We may want to debate who bears most blame for Jesus' death. Was it the Jewish religious leaders, who felt threatened because Jesus challenged their status? Was it the Roman governor, who feared he would lose his political appointment if the leaders reported him to Rome? Was it the crowds, who cried out to crucify Jesus? Each of these groups reflected a *me-first* attitude. Killing the One who revealed the *other-first* disposition was easier than changing their own attitudes. The world may attack us when we point out both its sin and its Redeemer. Proclaim both anyway.

TEACHING PLANS

Teaching Plan—Varied Learning Activities

Connect with Life

1. Play a round of "musical chairs." Arrange several chairs in a circle, one less than the number of people participating. Instruct the players to walk around behind the circle while someone plays music. When the music is stopped, everyone is to sit in a chair. Whoever is left without a chair is out of the game. As time permits, play a round or

two, removing a chair for each new round. Then, play another round or two, but this time, designate one player to pretend to be a wealthy person who came to the class to donate a large sum of money to someone. Have fun with the game but limit the time.

Upon completion, ask, *How did people behave in the first part of the game? Were people pushy or self-seeking?* Then ask, *How did people treat the "rich person" when he or she joined the game?* Finally, ask, *How do you think people would have treated a homeless person or a drug addict who joined the game?*

2. State that today's lesson will explore what Jesus taught his disciples about seeking personal greatness and serving others.

Guide Bible Study

3. Read Mark 9:30–32, and ask the class to listen for what Jesus was saying and how the disciples responded. Invite comments. Recall lesson eight briefly. Say, *We sometimes scorn the disciples for being dense. Can you think of a time when you were afraid to know more about something that was unpleasant or frightening?* Examples might include getting full information from a doctor about a diagnosed illness; and learning details of atrocities occurring in other parts of the world, or even about crime and corruption in the local community. Ask, *Why do people avoid comprehending unpleasant situations?*

4. Have someone read Mark 9:33–35. Ask, *Why do you think the disciples kept quiet when Jesus asked what they were talking about?* After responses, continue with this question: *What does Jesus' action of sitting down tell us?* Explain that sitting down suggested that Jesus wanted their full attention as he taught them something important.

5. Lead the class to brainstorm some people they consider "the greatest" at something. Consider areas such as sports, academics, entertainment, and science. Ask, *Aside from God-given ability, what are some things that generally are required to be "the greatest"?* (Answers should include hard work, intense focus, practice, etc.) Ask, *Are these qualities necessarily a bad thing? Is it wrong to seek greatness?* Allow time for discussion, and then ask, *Did Jesus condemn the disciples for their desire for greatness?* Note that Jesus did not condemn the desire, but he went on to teach them the godly way to become great.

UNIT THREE: With Jesus on the Way to the Cross

The Gospel of Mark: *Jesus' Works and Words*—Teaching Guide

6. Call attention to the illustration in the *Study Guide* under the heading "The Necessity of Humility" about Dr. Viktor Frankl. Invite the class to tell of times when they found joy, strength, or personal encouragement as they ministered to or helped another person. (You may want to break into groups of three or four for this exercise.)

7. Enlist someone to read Mark 9:35–37. State that children in that day were helpless and insignificant, considered to be among the very least important people. Ask, *What other kinds of groups or individuals were considered unimportant?* (Widows, orphans, lepers, and so on.) Ask, *Who are some people who are viewed as the least important in our society?* Accept several answers. Then ask, *Whom do you consider unimportant?* Allow time for private reflection.

Encourage Application

8. Ask: *What situations can you think of in today's world in which someone who is genuinely humble is highly praised? If we put Jesus' teachings about greatness into practice, what are some things that would change?*

9. In advance, prepare and copy these questions as a worksheet for each member. Leave space for answers. (A copy can be downloaded in "Teaching Resource Items" for this study from www.baptistwaypress.org.)

    - In what areas of my life do I seek greatness or wish I were great?
    - In what ways could my quest for greatness include or focus on service to others?
    - What are some practical steps I could take to serve others?
    - Whom do I need to welcome or accept as a way of welcoming Christ?

    Distribute the worksheets with pencils, and allow the class time to complete the activity. Close with prayer that each person will better understand and practice the connection between putting others before self and greatness in God's kingdom.

Teaching Plan—Lecture and Questions

Connect with Life

1. In advance, enlist a class member or someone else who is a manager of people in a job or volunteer situation. Interview this person with questions such as these:

   - What do the people who work for you do?
   - Who are your customers or clients?
   - How important is it for your organization and employees to provide service to customers or clients?
   - How do you get your workers to do their jobs and/or to provide service to customers?
   - Does your job require serving your workers? If so, how?

   Thank the person. Then ask whether anyone is familiar with the concept of a *servant leader.* Call for explanations of the concept. Note answers on the markerboard, or simply allow people to express their ideas.

2. Say, *In today's passage, we will see what Jesus taught his disciples about success through service and putting others ahead of oneself.*

Guide Bible Study

3. Review the incidents in Mark 9:1–29. Call attention to Jesus' transfiguration as described in Mark 9:1–8. Ask, *Do you think this experience changed the way Peter, John, and James viewed Jesus? How?*

4. Read Mark 9:30–32 while the class listens for Jesus' teaching. Ask, *Do you think Jesus' words were clear and straightforward? If so, why do you think the disciples "did not understand what he meant"* (NIV)? *Do you think Peter, James, and John were more or less confused than the other disciples?*

5. Have someone read Mark 9:33–34. Ask, *Why do we sometimes act as if the Lord is unaware of what we are doing or saying? How would we live our lives if we were more aware of Jesus' presence? How can we remind ourselves we are living in the presence of Jesus?* Continue by

asking, *What do you think being "the greatest" meant to the disciples? In what ways do people today (including ourselves) seek to be "the greatest"?* Lead the class to mention several areas of life. Note that being "the greatest" implies that other people must be less great.

6. Say, *Jesus used a little child to teach his lesson. What did the child represent?* Lead the class to brainstorm other individuals or groups who could represent the same helpless humility. Ask, *What are some ways people (including ourselves) fail to welcome these people? What are some concrete ways to welcome them? What connection do you see between being humble and a servant to all (9:36) and welcoming a little child (9:37)?*

Encourage Application

7. Invite the class to mention people they know or know about who are "great" in a quiet but service-oriented way.

8. Call attention to the small article "Applying Jesus' Teachings" in the *Study Guide*. Read through each entry. Note the third entry. Ask, *Can you think of some ways we push ourselves forward to try to get first place?* Accept several answers. Challenge the class to commit to being more aware of when and how they strive to be first in ways different from Jesus' teaching. Then ask, *Can you think of other ways beyond what is mentioned in this article by which we could serve other people around us?* Note the answers on the markerboard. Challenge the class to take action this week on some way of serving others.

Focal Text
Mark 10:32–45

Background
Mark 10:1–45

Main Idea
To be a genuine disciple of Jesus is to be a servant, not a master, of all.

Question to Explore
Are you a servant? How did you feel the last time someone treated you like one?

Teaching Aim
To lead the class to decide how they will respond as disciples to Jesus' teachings on servanthood

UNIT THREE

With Jesus on the Way to the Cross

Lesson Ten

Disciple = Servant

BIBLE COMMENTS

Understanding the Context

Between the second and third predictions of his passion (Mark 9:31; 10:33–34), Jesus' journey toward Jerusalem took him to Judea and Perea, the region referred to as "beyond the Jordan" (10:1). He resumed teaching the crowds after focusing on the Twelve in Galilee. He responded to questions regarding divorce and remarriage. He stressed the preciousness of children. He told a rich man that to inherit eternal life he needed to sell what he had, give the proceeds to the poor, and follow Jesus. The rich man walked sorrowfully away because he loved what he had and could not give it up. When Jesus warned the Twelve about riches, he promised that the reward for disciples exceeds what they give up to follow him. They would receive eternal life.

We may wonder why Jesus repeated the prediction of his suffering three times, but we must not forget the difficulty his followers had in understanding it. They struggled especially with the idea of a suffering Messiah. The emphasis in today's narrative is on the necessity of a disciple being a servant.

The disciples had showed glimmers of insight, such as when Peter confessed Jesus as the Christ (8:29). On the other hand, they continued to argue over who would be most important and prominent in Christ's kingdom. They could not cut their ties to worldly expectations. And the nearer they came to Jerusalem, the less they seemed to understand.

The request by James and John to be given places of prominence offers one of the most glaring examples of the disciples' misunderstanding of Jesus' concept of discipleship. Contrast their brashness and even arrogance with Jesus' concern for women who were the victims of divorce (10:1–12). Note how they lacked the childlikeness that was characteristic of those who would enter the kingdom of God (10:13–15). They were more like the rich man who discovered that money could not purchase eternal life than they were like the children Jesus blessed.

Jesus affirmed the two disciples' willingness to suffer but informed them that God alone could grant positions in the kingdom. He admonished them and the others by stressing that greatness was gained through serving others and not through worldly stature and recognition. Jesus pointed out that even the Son of Man came to serve and not be served. He became their ultimate example when he was nailed to a cross.

Interpreting the Scriptures

On the Road, Again (10:32)

Jesus and his followers continued their trek toward Jerusalem, which is named for the first time as the destination. Mark used "Jerusalem" figuratively as well as literally. The name evoked images of those who opposed Jesus, such as the chief priests (see 3:22; 7:1).

The picture of Jesus walking ahead of the travelers also suggests a figurative understanding as well as a literal one. Those who followed Jesus were both "amazed" and "fearful." The Twelve and others recognized Jesus' determination despite the growing hostility toward him. Mark's first readers might have found courage in Jesus' behavior. They were facing Roman persecution, and his example could have emboldened them to remain faithful. Jesus' walking ahead of them reminded his disciples again that he was the Master. Also, after Jesus' resurrection, the "young man" in the tomb commanded the women to tell the disciples that Jesus was "going ahead of" them to Galilee (16:5, 7). After Jesus' resurrection, he would still lead them.

Jesus' intent was clear. He was going to Jerusalem. We cannot know for certain how he knew what fate awaited him. Certainly previous encounters with religious leaders pointed to increasing hostility, with the likelihood of suffering and death.

Mark may have separated those who followed Jesus into two groups, one that was "amazed" and one that was "fearful." The "amazed" group might have been the Twelve, while those who were "fearful" composed a larger segment. This larger group may not have been as close to Jesus as the apostles but were still committed to following him as disciples.

What "amazed" Jesus' followers may have been his resolve. He controlled his own destiny. Anything that happened to him was because of divine directive. All the acts of his enemies were possible only because God allowed them (see 9:31). Jesus could have used his power to escape suffering and crucifixion. Different translations of "amazed" help understand the breadth of its meaning: "astonished" (NIV); "filled with awe" (New English Bible); "filled with alarm" (Today's English Version); and "were in a daze" (Jerusalem Bible). The second, and probably larger, group was frightened about what would occur in their future. Jesus again took the Twelve aside for private instruction.

A Third Passion Prediction (10:33–34)

Jesus added greater detail to each passion prediction. He announced in Mark 8:31 that he, the Messiah, would suffer. He added in Mark 9:31 the thought that he would be betrayed "into the hands of men." What's new in this final prediction is the mention of trial, scourging, and mocking. Jesus would be (1) "delivered over" to the Jewish leadership, (2) condemned to death, (3) handed over to the Gentiles, (4) taunted and scourged, (5) executed, and (6) resurrected. Jesus' words recall Old Testament passages in which an innocent person suffers harassment from others (Psalm 22:6–8; Isaiah 50:6).

Another element added to the passion predictions here is that the religious leaders would deliver Jesus over to the Gentiles. For Jews to collaborate with Gentiles stresses the contempt in which the authorities held Jesus.

The Request from James and John (10:35–40)

James and John, as well as the other disciples, remained clueless about what Jesus was trying to teach them. Three times Jesus had stressed that the Messiah, the Christ, would suffer and die. The Twelve continued to hear these words through the filter of victory and triumph as conceived by the world. Mark refused to gloss over this failure. He, of all the Gospel writers, may have been the harshest towards them. He did not remove their foibles but allowed his readers to see them as they were.

10:35–37. James and John were focused on the Messiah's glory (see Mark 8:38). They anticipated its coming and sought prominent places when it arrived. They approached Jesus to ask him for a favor, "to do for us whatever we ask of You."

What were they thinking when they posed this ambiguous question? Did they think Jesus would say *yes* before he knew what they wanted? Did they think they would receive special favors, perhaps because they were his cousins as some believe? Did they think that because they along with Peter were most intimate with him they would be given preference over the others? You might think they would have understood more fully what was happening, but not so. Who knows what they were thinking? Jesus refused to be entrapped and asked, "What do you want Me to do for you?" Their answer: "Grant that we may sit, one on Your right and one on Your left, in Your glory." The "right" and "left" indicate being next to the king in honor.

"In your glory' refers to Jesus' messianic glory (8:38). James and John apparently believed Jesus would receive his glory when they arrived in Jerusalem. Actually he did, but not as they envisioned it. Christ was glorified in his crucifixion. Note that Mark used the terms "the right" and "the left" one other time: to refer to the two who were crucified with Jesus (15:27).

10:38. James and John had no idea what they had asked for. Sharing Jesus' glory meant sharing his suffering. He asked whether they were able to participate with him in his "cup" and his "baptism." The question implies the answer is *no*. "Cup" symbolizes suffering and may anticipate Jesus' prayer in the Garden of Gethsemane: "Remove this cup from Me" (14:36). "Baptism" denotes being immersed in affliction and may suggest Jesus needed to die in this life to be raised to eternal life. Jesus' disciples could expect that the fate that awaited him awaited them.

The two disciples maintained that they could participate with Jesus in his suffering. I imagine Jesus tenderly looking at them, contemplating what lay ahead, and replying that they would indeed experience that suffering. However, the positions they sought were not his to give. The statement, "it is for those for whom it has been prepared," indicates that God alone determined who would sit on Jesus' right and left. Jesus could not offer these positions. Certain things were determined and known by the Father alone, such as this and the time of Jesus' Second Coming (13:32).

The Other Disciples' Resentment (10:41)

Hearing the request from James and John angered the other disciples. Jesus' reply suggests that what upset them was that the brothers had asked Jesus for the positions before they did. Mark used their reaction to link all the disciples together and to reinforce the persistent misunderstanding of all of them.

True Greatness (10:42–45)

10:42. The disciples' understanding of greatness was the same as the Gentiles' concept of power. The world equates power and greatness with exercising control over others. For Jesus to compare their understanding of power to the Gentiles must have jolted the Twelve.

10:43–44. Jesus did not condemn the disciples' desire to be great but redefined greatness according to his kingdom. Great people seek to serve and not control. These two verses are a type of poetry in which the second verse (10:44) parallels the first (10:43). The word "servant" designates one who waits on tables and occupies a low position in society. Those who would be great would be "slave of all." A slave was owned by another and had no rights unless granted by the owner.

10:45. Jesus set himself up as an example for the kind of servanthood that produced greatness. He expected this type of behavior from his disciples. Mark's readers already recognized that Jesus was the divine Son of God (1:1). If anybody deserves to be served by others, it is God. However Jesus, the Son of God, came to serve and not to be served.

Jesus stated the purpose for his coming as being "to give His life a ransom for many." Understanding "ransom" is central to interpreting what Jesus meant.

UNIT THREE: With Jesus on the Way to the Cross

The word "ransom" appears in the gospels only here and in Matthew 20:28. Similar words such as *redeem* and *redemption* are found throughout the New Testament. A "ransom" was a price paid for purchasing the release of either a prisoner of war or a slave. The Old Testament emphasizes the freedom that follows and the restoration of relationship (see Exodus 21:30; Leviticus 25:51–52; Numbers 18:15).

"Ransom" also suggests substitution. Many interpreters see an allusion to Isaiah's suffering servant (Isaiah 53:1–6), who offered himself in place of others. Jesus fit this description perfectly.

Another facet of "ransom" was its cost. While this concept may be included here, in most cases the emphasis falls more on the ensuing freedom than the price. In Jesus' case, the cost for redeeming humanity was his life. The word does not suggest that the ransom was paid to anyone or anything. Jesus did not pay a "ransom" to any power of evil to secure redemption.

Jesus gave his life "for many." "Many" here is used in the Jewish manner, thus meaning *all*. It means multitude as opposed to an individual. The preposition "for" usually means *instead of* but can also mean *in behalf of*. Jesus' death provided redemption for all humanity, something people could not do for themselves.

Focusing on the Meaning

Disciples, then and now, follow Jesus despite not fully understanding him and realizing the danger involved. We may cringe when we think how slow the disciples were to understand that discipleship means suffering. Let's not be too harsh on them. They stayed with Jesus until his arrest. Too, although they fell away, they were restored and continued Jesus' work. Disciples in every age struggle with fear and lack of understanding.

God's values differ from worldly values. People tend to seek positions for glory and power. We have been bombarded with these values from birth. Overcoming these long-seated perceptions is difficult. We see far too much of ourselves in the request from James and John. We can learn from the disciples that a divine purpose for our lives can replace worldly ambitions.

Following Christ and his example is the best way to become great in God's eyes. Focus not on greatness but on service, and you will be great. As Jesus served and gave himself for others, so should we. We have been bought with a price. We should glorify God in all we do.

Observing the Lord's Supper and baptism reminds us of Jesus' suffering and the privilege and responsibility we have to share this with him. Because Jesus used the terms "cup" and "baptism" for his passion, every time we observe the Lord's Supper or witness the ordinance of baptism we are reminded of the necessity of suffering. To participate in the ordinances and through them in Jesus' life is to commit ourselves to participate in Jesus' suffering.

TEACHING PLANS

Teaching Plan—Varied Learning Activities

Connect with Life

1. In as convincing a manner as you can manage, say that your church has asked your class to take on the responsibility of building maintenance for the next three months. The class will need to organize itself to do groundskeeping (mowing, etc.); to clean the sanctuary, classrooms, and hallways; to scrub the restrooms; and to prepare and clean up for all coffee service or other types of meals. Ask for volunteers to help with the specific tasks. After a few minutes, reveal that this is just an exercise. Ask, *How did you feel about the class assignment? How did you feel about the prospect of doing these kinds of things for the church?*

2. Say, *Our lesson today continues Jesus' teaching about the importance of humility and selfless service for true disciples.*

Guide Bible Study

3. Divide the class into three groups. Each group is to compare a passage in this week's lesson with a passage in last week's lesson. Assign group one to compare Mark 9:30–32 with 10:32–34. Assign group two Mark 9:33–34 and 10:35–37. Assign group three to study Mark 9:36–37 and 10:13–16. Explain that the reports should be brief and

The Gospel of Mark: Jesus' Works and Words—Teaching Guide

should identify similarities and differences between the assigned passages. Allow a few minutes for work, and then call for reports. (Encourage participants to stay in their groups for the activity in step 4.) Then ask, *Why do you think Mark included these passages that seem similar?*

4. Again working in small groups, assign each group to dramatize Mark 10:32–37. Groups may rephrase the words of Jesus, James, and John to reflect modern language and images. After a few minutes, call for performances.

   Note that the *Study Guide* uses the subtitle "Blinded by Personal Ambition" to describe the disciples in this passage. Ask, *What or who are some other examples of people (or literary characters) being blinded by ambition?*

   Read the next-to-last paragraph in the *Study Guide* section, "Blinded by Personal Ambition," and 2 Corinthians 12:1–10. Ask, *Can you think of a time when you have been tempted by personal ambition? Do you feel God has used circumstances in your life as a "thorn in the flesh"?* Allow private reflection, or call for answers.

5. Enlist someone to read Mark 10:38–39. Ask, *What do you think James and John thought Jesus meant in verse 38?* Note that "baptism" did not necessarily mean what it does to Christians today; rather, it implied more of a shared experience. Lead a discussion with questions such as these: *What "cup" and "baptism" are Christian believers asked to share with Jesus in our day? What is your personal "cup" and "baptism"? Are you prepared to answer as confidently as James and John in verse 39? Why? What does it take to endure the same experience as Jesus did?* Continue by asking, *How do you feel about Jesus' statement in Mark 10:40?*

6. Read Mark 10:41–42. Call for examples of prominent people in today's world who demand special treatment and privilege. Think of people in sports, entertainment, business, politics, or the church.

7. Explain (or review from last week's lesson) the concept of *servant leadership*. Call for examples of people in today's world who practice *servant leadership*.

8. Refer to the small article, "Servant," in the *Study Guide*. Stress that the word *diakonos* (servant) is used in Mark 10:43, but *doulos* (slave) is used in verse 44. Ask, *How do we feel about the terms or concepts*

Lesson 10: Disciple = Servant

associated with "slave" versus "servant"? Why do you you think Jesus used the terms?

Encourage Application

9. Refer the class to the small article in the *Study Guide*, "Naming Rights." Divide the class into two teams, or select volunteers for two teams, and debate the two sides of the issue. Allow a few minutes for the groups to organize their thoughts. Each side should be allowed about two minutes to present their case and then one minute to present a rebuttal to the other side's argument. At the end of the debate, regardless of which side argued more strongly, ask, *What do you think Jesus would say, especially in light of this passage of Scripture?*

10. Note that the Scripture passage has dealt with *service, self-sacrifice,* and *humility*, and write these words on the markerboard. Ask, *How much do you think these qualities are valued in our society? Are they qualities we find in ourselves?*

    Conclude by asking, *How would you evaluate yourself on these qualities?* Allow time for silent reflection and prayer.

Teaching Plan—Lecture and Questions

Connect with Life

1. State that all of us have people in our lives whom we serve, and people who serve us. On the markerboard, make two columns labeled "People We Serve," and "People Who Serve Us." Call for examples of each and write them in the respective columns.

    Review the lists, and ask, *How do we feel about being servants? How do we feel about serving others?* Take a few minutes for answers and discussion.

2. Say, *In today's lesson, we will learn more about how Jesus taught and set the ultimate example about how Christians are to live lives that serve others.*

Guide Bible Study

3. Briefly review the background passage, Mark 10:1–31. Call attention to the challenging messages and commands Jesus gave his listeners regarding divorce (10:1–13), humility (10:13–16), and worldly wealth (10:17–31).

4. Read 10:32. Ask, *Why do you think the disciples were "astonished," and some who followed "were afraid"* (NIV)?

5. Enlist someone to read 10:33–34. Lead the class to compare Jesus' words to those in Mark 9:31. Ask, *Why do you think Jesus was more detailed and explicit in predicting his death in 10:33–34?*

6. Read Mark 10:35–40. Guide discussion by asking these questions:
   - What does it mean to sit at the right or left hand (10:37, 40)?
   - How do you explain the request of James and John in view of Jesus' words in Mark 10:33–34?
   - Are there times when we hear a difficult but clear teaching of Jesus and either ignore it, misunderstand it, or change the subject?

   Explain "cup" and "baptism" in Mark 10:38–39. Ask, *How should Christian believers feel about sharing in Jesus' cup and baptism?*

7. Invite someone to read Mark 10:41–44. Summarize the small article, "As a Ransom," in the *Study Guide.* Add insights from "Bible Comments" in this *Teaching Guide.* Ask, *Do you think the disciples were able to relate these words of Jesus to his prediction of his death (10:33–34)?* State, *Jesus literally "gave his life" in service to humankind. In North America today, it is most unlikely that Christians will have to die for their faith. Even so, how can Christian believers today follow Jesus' example of giving their lives in service to the Lord?*

Encourage Application

8. Lead a discussion using the questions at the end of the lesson in the *Study Guide.* Also ask: *Are Christians obligated to act as servants in their secular environments (for example, at work, school, community, or*

home)? Should they make it a point to explain they are acting as servants because of their Christian conviction? Why?

9. Explain that the word "disciple" usually means a student or pupil. For the disciples in the Gospels, Jesus was the Teacher or Master. Say, *Our lesson title is "Disciple = Servant." Is it true that people learn by serving?* Call for examples, including personal experience. Then ask, *What did Jesus teach about serving by the example he set?*

10. Conclude by asking the class to reflect prayerfully on this question: *How will you respond to Jesus' teachings in this passage, especially in light of what Jesus did for you?*

Focal Text

Mark 13:1–13, 32–37

Background

Mark 13

Main Idea

When disciples face opposition and even the threat of death, they are to continue to be faithful witnesses for Jesus, relying on the Spirit's power.

Question to Explore

How far should we really be willing to go for this Christianity thing?

Teaching Aim

To lead the class to evaluate the seriousness of their commitment to Jesus and to commit themselves to being faithful

UNIT THREE

With Jesus on the Way to the Cross

Lesson Eleven

Discipleship in Dangerous Times

BIBLE COMMENTS

Understanding the Context

When we last encountered Jesus, he was teaching the apostles that greatness consisted in serving others. He had predicted for the third and final time his suffering, death, and resurrection (Mark 10:32–34). His instruction in the true meaning of discipleship remained the same: Disciples would suffer as he suffered.

The next event Mark recorded was an act of service by Jesus. He healed Bartimaeus as he passed through Jericho on his way to Jerusalem (10:46–52).

The crowds had hailed Jesus as king as he entered Jerusalem (11:1–10). The background for this is found in 1 Kings 1:32–40. David had designated Solomon his successor. David commanded his aides to lead his son into the city on the king's colt. Jesus followed a route that was similar if not identical to the one Solomon had taken.

Passion week was a busy time for Jesus. The tension between Jesus and the religious leaders intensified. He spent a great deal of his time in the temple. He drove money changers and merchants from its outer court. While Jesus taught there, the chief priests, scribes, and elders challenged his authority (Mark 11:27–28). Pharisees and Herodians, two groups at opposite ends of the political spectrum, joined together to entrap Jesus. They asked whether Jews should pay taxes to Caesar (12:13–17). Sadducees disputed his teachings on the resurrection (12:18–27). He commended a woman who gave but two copper coins as an offering (12:38–44). At this time Mark's account moves from Jesus in the temple to a private conversation of Jesus with his disciples on the Mount of Olives.

A second context for interpreting Mark 13 concerns the burdens Jesus' disciples were bearing when Mark was written. This conversation on the Mount of Olives would have encouraged disheartened and troubled disciples at that time. Mark offered these words to bring strength and hope to his readers.

Mark 13 has been called "The Little Apocalypse." Apocalyptic literature, including Daniel and Revelation, was written during times of persecution to encourage God's people. Apocalyptic literature offers assurance for facing the future when the world has caved in. Characteristics of apocalyptic literature include a pessimism regarding the world; anticipation of the end; visions that were often grotesque; and cosmic events, such as stars falling from the sky or the sun scorching the earth. Mark included no grotesque imagery in this chapter, but we can see the other traits. The title for today's lesson, "Discipleship in Dangerous Times," provides a good description for apocalyptic literature.

Interpreting the Scriptures

Mark 13 interrupts the narrative flow of the Gospel as Jesus has moved ever nearer to the cross. As Jesus left the temple for the last time, one of the disciples made a seemingly innocent comment that sparked Jesus' longest discourse in Mark's Gospel (13:5–37).

Not One Stone Unturned (13:1–4)

13:1. The temple was the religious center of Judaism. Many Jews would save money all their lives to make one trip to worship in Jerusalem.

The temple was a magnificent work of architecture. Its courtyard covered as much as twenty-six acres. Its beauty and grandeur were stunning. The sanctuary itself was built of white stone with intricate carvings. Parts were inlaid with gold. The massive "stones" were thirty-seven feet long by twelve feet high by eighteen feet deep and evoked a sense of stability and security. The disciple's comment in 13:1 reflected the honor given the temple by Jews.

13:2. Jesus' reply surely shocked the disciples: "Not one stone will be left upon another." The temple in Jesus' day was the third one in Israel's history. Solomon built the first, which the Babylonians destroyed in 586 B.C. Zerubbabel rebuilt it after the Jews returned from Babylonian exile. Herod the Great began the work on the third temple, the temple of New Testament times, to gain favor with the Jews. The project was still in progress when the Romans destroyed the temple in A.D. 70.

The words "do you see" suggest taking a reflective look at the temple. The words may imply a slight rebuke, for, according to one interpretation, Jesus was denouncing the barrenness of Jewish worship, which was symbolized by the temple. At the very least Jesus' words spoke of the temple's impermanence. That "not one stone will be left upon another" underscores the temple's complete devastation. More devastating than the destruction of the building would be the people's emotional loss, which can be compared to the loss citizens of the United States felt when the twin towers in New York City were destroyed.

13:3–4. Jesus and the disciples had crossed the Kidron valley to the "Mount of Olives," which offered a marvelous view of the temple. Peter, Andrew, James, and John continued to question Jesus about his statement. These four, whom Jesus chose first (1:16–20), had stayed with him through some difficult times. Mark may have singled these out to stress that they would be restored despite abandoning Jesus soon after this conversation. Christians in Mark's day would find encouragement in knowing that although Jesus' closest companions had failed him, he restored them (see John 21:15–19).

As Jesus and the disciples looked across the valley from the Mount of Olives to the temple, Old Testament associations between the two may have inspired the questions in verse 4. The apostles' two questions are really one, for both refer to the destruction of the temple. The apostles wanted to know when these events would occur. What signs would indicate that the time was approaching?

Including the word "all" in the second question may indicate that the apostles realized that Jesus was talking about more than the ruin of the temple. The word "fulfilled" (*accomplished*) denotes achievement or finality.

Signs (13:5–8)

Jesus did not answer their question directly because he was more concerned that they would have the strength to face the difficult times than when they would occur. The numerous imperative verbs that appear in Mark 13:5–37 make it obvious that Jesus was giving practical teaching about how to remain faithful in difficult times.

13:5–6. "See to it" (*watch*) is the first word in Jesus' reply. Similar verbs, "be on your guard" (13:9); "take heed" (13:23, 33); and "be on the alert" (13:35, 37) appear in the text.

Jesus warned them that false prophets would appear. "In My name" likely denotes the false prophets' false claim that Jesus had sent them. The phrase may suggest that these claimed Messianic power and were coming to set things right in the world. The words "I am He" hint that some of the false messiahs were claiming to be divine.

13:7–8. The various "signs" Jesus mentioned had been used previously by God in dealings with people. God had used wars, earthquakes, and famines to accomplish divine purposes (see Isaiah 19:2; Judges 5:4–5; Psalm 18:7–8; Isa. 24:19; Jeremiah 15:2; Ezekiel 5:17).

Disciples would hear of wars and rumors of war. They would have firsthand knowledge of some of these, such as the fall of Jerusalem. They would hear reports of others. "Wars" were often associated with the end times in Jewish literature. Because wars were inevitable, they could not be used to predict. Too, because they were inevitable, disciples were not to fear when they came. God had not deserted the disciples. Events in human history would not determine when Christ would reappear or diminish his concerns for his followers.

Jesus then pointed out the certainty of two natural catastrophes: earthquakes and famines. Again, neither of these would predict Jesus' return. Along with wars, these would show that Jesus' disciples would experience agonizing times.

Jesus associated these disasters with the "beginning of birth pangs." "Birth pangs" were a symbol of God's judgment (Jeremiah 6:24; Micah 4:10).

UNIT THREE: With Jesus on the Way to the Cross

Expect Opposition (13:9–13)

Disciples ought to be more concerned about the opposition to them than about natural calamities. The repeated use of "you" in this section stresses Jesus' care for his followers.

13:9. The section is joined by the use of one word translated in three ways: "deliver" (13:9); "arrest and hand you over" (13:11); and "betray" (13:12). Jesus warned his followers to "be on your guard" for their opponents would "deliver you to the courts." "Delivered" can mean either *betrayed* or *arrested*. *Betrayed* would indicate action by people whom they trusted, while *arrested* denoted activity by their enemies.

The "courts" were local bodies found in each Jewish community. Jewish authorities would punish Jesus' disciples by whipping them. "Governors and kings" were non-Jewish authorities, who grew more and more antagonistic to the church. Christians would face both Jewish and Roman hostility because of their faithfulness to Christ ("for My sake").

13:10–11. Jesus stressed the importance of preaching the gospel even though such proclamation would increase the animosity toward the disciples. Like other *signs* in this chapter, this verse should not be used to attempt to predict when Jesus will return. Use it instead to stress the need to persevere in serving while suffering.

Jesus instructed his followers to focus on proclamation. They did not need to prepare to defend themselves before the authorities, for the Holy Spirit would provide them with what to say in their defense.

13:12–13. Note the widespread hostility the disciples would face. Family members would turn on one another. Jesus declared: "you will be hated by all."

Jesus offered this encouragement: "The one who endures to the end, he will be saved." To "be saved" means to have an abiding relationship with Christ. "End" refers to the time when a person's life on earth ceases, whether at death or at Christ's return.

Watchfulness (13:32–37)

13:32. The Father alone knows the time ("that day") the Son of Man will return.

LESSON 11: Discipleship in Dangerous Times

13:33. Jesus urged the disciples to "keep on the alert." This is the only time in Mark's Gospel where this verb is used. It suggests vigilance. "Appointed time" means an appropriate time set by God and not chronological time. Readiness, not prediction, is again the focus.

13:34–36. Jesus told a parable to illustrate the importance of watchfulness. A man who was traveling had left home and assigned each of his servants a task. They were to carry out their work faithfully without undue concern as to when he would return. They were to be prepared at any moment for his arrival and not try to guess when that would be. The terms "evening," "midnight," "rooster crows," and "in the morning" are all technical terms for watches during the night. They emphasize that one should be constantly attentive to one's assigned work.

13:37. Jesus concluded this discourse as he had launched it: "Be on the alert." We might say, be prepared at every moment.

Focusing on the Meaning

Disciples ought first to listen to Jesus. I hear people claim the Bible has answers for all our questions. When we approach the Bible in that way, I fear that we've missed out on a great deal of what's significant. We ought to let Jesus ask, and then answer, the important questions. Look at the disciples. Jesus didn't answer the question they asked about when the end would come. He answered the question they should have asked: *How should we live in a world that seeks to harm Christians?*

False messiahs appear in different forms. Two quickly come to mind: nationalism and institutional religion. We live in trying times. A glance at the daily news reveals wars and rumors of wars, famines, and earthquakes, along with corruption in business and government, widespread poverty around the world, and rampant uneasiness. Voters align themselves behind candidates who promise security and certainty. We trust armies to protect us from terrorists. We flock to churches looking for God to make things better when times get tough. Don't forget that serving Christ may increase our struggles. Remain committed to proclaiming the gospel that Jesus is the only Messiah who offers true deliverance.

Disciples should focus on proclamation, not on defending themselves. Our world needs the good news of Jesus, the Son of God. Don't hunker down in foxholes. Don't hide behind church walls. Christians in every age suffer persecution. Don't become preoccupied with hardships. Be faithful to the work to which you were called. Focus on Jesus' mission, and the Holy Spirit will provide strength and guidance when needed.

Thinking about Christ's return has a proper place in disciples' lives. Using your calendar (or PDA) in connection with Jesus' anticipated return is good, if you use them to schedule ministry and not to pencil (don't use pen) in dates for his Second Coming.

In summary: Remain faithful to Christ in difficult times. He is faithful to deliver.

TEACHING PLANS

Teaching Plan—Varied Learning Activities

Connect with Life

1. Ask, *Is there anyone here—or does anyone know anyone—who has ever been afraid that being a Christian would require doing something unpleasant, uncomfortable, inconvenient, or scary?* Probe for answers, which could include fears of going on overseas missions to dangerous lands, giving up a carefree lifestyle, facing ridicule from acquaintances or family, and so on. Then ask, *Have any of these fears come to pass?*

2. Say, *Although most people's worst fears about following Christ seldom materialize, no one can say we will be spared pain and trouble. Jesus himself said, "In this world you will have trouble"* (John 16:33, NIV). *Today we will explore what Jesus taught his disciples, including each of us, to expect in their lives and in the future.*

Guide Bible Study

3. Briefly review the events of Jesus' entry to Jerusalem and his ministry in the city (Mark 11—12). Note that the events in this passage are within the last week of Jesus' life.

Read Mark 13:1–4 aloud while the class listens for the exchange between Jesus and the disciples. Invite comments on how the disciples must have felt after Jesus' response in verse 2.

4. Divide into two groups. Group one is to search Mark 13:5–13 for the events and occurrences to which Jesus referred. Group two is to search Mark 13:5–13 for Jesus' commands and instructions to his disciples. (If more than twelve people are present, form additional groups with duplicate assignments so that groups will have no more than six people in them.) Each group should make a list—perhaps on paper or a markerboard—of their findings. As a whole group, review each list and summarize. Stress that Jesus predicted calamities that were of both natural and human origin, plus personal opposition. He also insisted that disciples stay alert, not worry, and stand firm as they bear witness to the gospel.

    Ask, *What are some common situations where people like us are fearful to express their faith in Jesus Christ? Why are we so fearful? What messages do we see in this passage that could encourage us?*

5. Read Mark 13:14–23. Point out that this passage most likely refers to the Roman destruction of Jerusalem, in A.D. 66–70, and that many of Jesus' listeners did witness the horrific events. Then read Mark 13:24–31 and state that this passage most likely refers to the future Second Coming of Christ and uses picturesque language that would have been very familiar and meaningful to the Jews of Jesus' day.

    Say, *I assume you have a lot of questions. We won't even attempt to answer them, but let's note the questions we can come up with.* After noting the questions, ask, *What do you think was the intent of Jesus' words?*

6. Ask, *What does it mean to live "in the last days"?* After accepting answers, review the small article in the *Study Guide*, "When? What Should I Do?" Enlist someone to read Mark 13:32–37 while the class listens for what they think is the main point. Ask, *What would happen if we knew exactly when Christ was returning? How would you live differently?*

Encourage Application

7. Refer the class to the small article in the *Study Guide*, "Case Study." Divide the class into small groups of no more than six people each. Allow a few minutes for each group to read the case study and develop their advice to Betsy. Call for reports.

8. Divide into groups of two or three. Read 1 Peter 3:15. Say, *What would you tell someone about your hope and faith in Jesus Christ, and what reasons would you give?* End with prayer.

Teaching Plan—Lecture and Questions

Connect with Life

1. Either tell or invite someone else to tell the incident at the beginning of the lesson in the *Study Guide* about the young boy who professed his faith in Christ. Recall recent news accounts of Christians suffering persecution in various parts of the world.[1] Before continuing, pause to pray for people around the world who are suffering for their Christian faith.

2. Then say, *Although few if any of us will ever face this kind of persecution, we can be certain we will encounter pain and trouble in life. Will we be able to maintain our Christian faith? Today's lesson will help us be prepared.*

Guide Bible Study

3. Briefly review the events of Jesus' entry to Jerusalem and his ministry in the city (Mark 11—12; see "Understanding the Context" in this *Teaching Guide*). Note that the events in this passage are within the last week of Jesus' life.

    Read Mark 13:1–4 while the class listens for what impressed the disciples and how Jesus responded. Present a mini-lecture on the temple in Jerusalem, including its history, size, and splendor, using the information on 13:1–4 in this *Teaching Guide*. Ask, *Why would the disciples be alarmed to hear Jesus say the temple would be destroyed?*

4. Read Mark 13:5–13. State that some Bible scholars hold this entire passage—all the way to Mark 13:31—to be a description of the destruction of Jerusalem in A. D. 70. Others think it describes the distant future and the Second Coming of Christ. Still others believe it pertains to both. Regardless, we can view it as a picture of the kinds of troubles Christians can expect to witness. Ask, *What directions or commands do you see in this passage?* Write responses on the board as you lead the class through the verses, identifying the imperatives from Jesus to the disciples.

5. Explain that Mark 13:14–31 uses "apocalyptic" language, characterized by rich imagery, symbolism, uncertain timing, and other features (see "Understanding the Context" in this *Teaching Guide*). The precise meaning of this passage has challenged Bible scholars for centuries. Next, tell the class to close their eyes as you read the verses. Ask, *What kind of pictures or images does the passage create? Without being certain of the details, what is your general sense of the passage? Who is in control of the events?* Finally, ask, *What effect does it have on believers dealing with uncertainties in life if they believe the Lord is in control of the immediate as well as the distant future?*

6. Invite someone to read Mark 13:32–37. Ask, *What seems to have been the most pressing question the disciples had? Why do you think Jesus emphasized the timing was completely unknown, except to God? What can "keep watch" mean to believers today? What do you think Jesus' main message to the disciples was? How does that apply to us?*

7. Lead a discussion using the questions provided in the *Study Guide*.

Encourage Application

8. Ask, *What are some examples of difficulties or disasters Christians can expect to face in life?* Allow the class to generate a list. Include "persecution" and "martyrdom." State that none of us knows what difficulties or disasters we will have to face in the future, and believers can and do become discouraged about their faith in desperate situations. Ask, *How can remembering Jesus' words about being on guard, not worrying, standing firm, and depending on the Holy Spirit help believers as they face desperate situations?*

The Gospel of Mark: *Jesus' Works and Words*—Teaching Guide

9. Read the illustration about the clay flowerpots in the fourth paragraph in the section "Faithful in the Face of Suffering" in the *Study Guide*. Ask, *What has been a "kiln" in your life, a difficult time that even so has helped strengthen your faith? What has that experience taught you about what you need to do as you face challenges?* You can take answers from the group or allow them to break into pairs or small groups to discuss. Invite the class to commit or re-commit themselves to serving Christ in spite of any difficulties they face in doing so. Close with a prayer of thanks that God has anticipated our pains, fears, and struggles in life and given us assurance about facing them with faith.

NOTES

1. Check www.bwanet.org, the website of the Baptist World Alliance.

Lesson 11: Discipleship in Dangerous Times

Lesson Twelve

Not Me

Focal Text
Mark 14:10–31

Background
Mark 14:1–31

Main Idea
We are to live in complete faithfulness to Jesus, remembering that he gave his life for us.

Question to Explore
How can we avoid failing to be faithful to Jesus?

Teaching Aim
To lead the class to explain the significance of the Lord's Supper and to state how it encourages faithful discipleship

UNIT THREE

With Jesus on the Way to the Cross

BIBLE COMMENTS

Understanding the Context

Mark resumed his account of Jesus' passion after Jesus had completed his conversation with the disciples concerning faithfulness in dangerous times (Mark 13:1–37). The stakes were high. His death was imminent. Mark 14 describes how various groups and individuals were preparing for Jesus' death.

One group was preparing to silence Jesus. The story picks up with the chief priests and scribes seeking to arrest him without causing a riot among the people (14:1–2). These leaders remembered how the crowds had welcomed him as he entered Jerusalem the previous Sunday (11:1–10). They felt threatened by Jesus' popularity.

A woman was preparing for Jesus' burial (14:3–9). One night after a busy day in the temple, Jesus was eating in Bethany at the home of Simon the leper. The woman interrupted the meal and anointed Jesus' head with precious perfume. Some who observed her act criticized it as irresponsible. She could have sold the oil and used the money to provide for the poor. Jesus reprimanded those who complained. They could always care for the poor.

The Lord commended the woman, declaring that she was anointing him prior to his burial.

Perhaps she realized more than any other person how near Jesus was to his death. She had to act then or the time would be too late. Her honoring Jesus would be remembered by those who heard the good news preached.

Judas Iscariot would be remembered as the one who betrayed Jesus. His preparations were those of a traitor as he plotted with religious leaders to turn Jesus over to them.

Jesus prepared for his death by instituting a memorial supper to remind his followers of his faithfulness to them and to his mission. The devotion of Jesus' disciples to him in our day, too, will determine how faithful they remain to him in difficult times. Our participation in that commemorative supper affords us encouragement and strength to remain faithful to him. Our devotion grows as we share the bread and drink from the cup.

Interpreting the Scriptures

Judas's Treachery (14:10–11)

Mark again used what we might call *bookends* for emphasis. That is, the description of the woman's act in 14:3–9 comes between the scheming of the religious leaders in 14:1–2 and Judas's treachery in 14:10–11.

14:10. We know little about "Judas Iscariot" (literally, *Judas from Kerioth*). The biblical account offers little information about his motive. Matthew's Gospel seems to imply greed (Matthew 26:14), and the Gospel of John speaks of his being a thief (John 12:1–6). Both Luke and John speak of Satan entering into him (Luke 22:3; John 13:26–27). Mark simply notes that the authorities gave him money in return for his participation.

Interpreters have speculated about motives for Judas's betraying Jesus. One suggested motive is personal ambition. Some claim Judas was disappointed that Jesus believed the Messiah was a suffering servant and not a military savior. Thus Judas hoped his actions would force Jesus' hand so Jesus would lead his people to political freedom. Mentioning that Judas was one of the Twelve further underscores the treacherousness of his act.

14:11. The religious authorities were elated when Judas offered to help them. They wanted to seize Jesus without creating a disturbance among the crowds gathered in Jerusalem to celebrate Passover. An "opportune time" would be one when they could secretly arrest Jesus.

Preparation for the Passover Meal (14:12–16)

14:12. The next morning Jesus sent two disciples into Jerusalem to prepare the Passover meal. Preparation for the Passover meal consisted of arranging the room where it would be eaten. Jewish law required that the meal be eaten within Jerusalem. Residents of the city were expected to and did provide rooms for pilgrims. Preparation also included baking the unleavened bread, mixing the sauce, and killing and roasting the Passover lamb.

14:13. Jesus sent Peter and John (Luke 22:8) into the city to make arrangements. They would find a man carrying a clay water pitcher.

14:14–16. The two disciples were to follow the man, who would lead them to a house. They were to inform the owner of the house that the "Teacher" was seeking the "guest room" where he would eat the Passover meal with his disciples. Jesus seems to have planned these actions in advance to minimize his public appearances in Jerusalem. Note that Jesus called this "My guest room," which indicates one he had reserved in advance.

The "large upper room" was located on the roof of the house and could be reached by outside stairs. "Furnished" suggests that the room was prepared with a low center table surrounded by cushions on which the diners could recline. The table may already have been set as well. Verse 16 records that everything occurred as Jesus had said.

Prediction of Betrayal (14:17–21)

14:17. After sundown Jesus and the Twelve entered Jerusalem and went to the upper room to eat the Passover meal. Passover commemorated God's deliverance of the Israelites from Egyptian slavery. Celebrants hoped God would soon intervene in their history again. Jesus understood this intervention would occur through his suffering and death.

14:18. Jesus and the Twelve were reclining on their left sides with their heads toward the table. Their legs extended outward, like spokes on a wheel. During this joyous time, Jesus shattered the festive mood by announcing that one of them would betray him. His words alluded to Psalm 41:9 and heightened the treachery of Judas's act. Table fellowship implies a relationship of trust, forgiveness, friendship, and intimacy.

14:19. To think that one of the Twelve would betray Jesus shocks us. What may be more jolting is that each of the Twelve wondered whether he would be the culprit. The question "surely not I" expected a negative answer. They were looking for Jesus to reassure them they would not be the guilty one. Each one realized that, in some situations, they were capable of disowning him.

14:20. Jesus did not identify the traitor. Instead he accented the supposed intimacy between the traitor and himself. They had shared fellowship and food. They had dipped together "in the bowl."

14:21. Jesus knew the events that were occurring were part of God's plan ("written of Him"). That the events were determined by God did not excuse Judas. Jesus condemned his involvement ("woe to that man"). Jesus stressed the depth of the tragedy of Judas's life by adding the statement that it would have been "good for that man if he had not been born."

Institution of the Lord's Supper (14:22–25)

14:22. The Passover meal followed a strict order. It began with the head of the family offering a prayer of thanksgiving followed by drinking a cup of wine. The main course was then served. Before it was eaten, the host offered a blessing for the bread, broke it, and offered a piece to the participants. During the eating of the main meal, they would pause when a son would ask the father why Passover night differed from all others. The father would narrate the Exodus story, after which they would sing psalms of praise (Psalms 114—118) and drink a second cup of wine. Another prayer of thanks was offered, a third cup was shared, and the eating of the main meal resumed. The meal ended by midnight with singing of more psalms and drinking a fourth and final cup.

Jesus reinterpreted the Passover meal for his disciples in light of his redemptive work. He took a piece of bread during the eating of the main course ("while they were eating") and broke it. This was the point at which the host offered the blessing for the bread. As Jesus distributed the bread to them, he said of it, "This is My body." We should understand "is" to mean *represents*. The distributing of the bread is what should be emphasized. He was promising the Twelve his abiding presence in their lives. They would rely heavily on that promise.

14:23–24. Jesus' taking the cup coincided with the third cup of the meal. Drinking the cup had clear sacrificial connotations. To call it "the blood of the covenant" associated it with Exodus 24:8: "So Moses took the blood and sprinkled it on the people, and said, 'Behold the blood of the covenant, which the Lord has made with you in accordance with all these words.'" Some translations include the word "new" before "covenant," but many ancient manuscripts omit it. (Luke 22:20 includes "new.") The meaning is clearly present, as is the allusion to the new covenant of Jeremiah 31:31–34. Jesus' death, symbolized by blood, sealed the covenant he was making with his disciples.

Using the term "cup" rather than *wine* is significant. "Cup" referred to Jesus' suffering the two other times Mark used it (Mark 10:38–39). It symbolizes both his death and the salvation accomplished through his death.

14:25. Jesus knew this meal was the last he would share with his disciples before his death. He likely spoke the words of this verse just before the time for drinking the fourth cup "of the fruit of the vine." He would drink with them again, but only after he had accomplished his redemptive mission. The statement is one of triumph.

A Last Warning (14:26–31)

14:26–27. Jesus and his disciples went to the Mount of Olives after finishing the meal. There Jesus predicted they would be scattered in the approaching hours.

The reference to striking "down the shepherd" comes from Zechariah 13:7. In that passage, God's smiting the shepherd was an essential part of the process through which God formed a new people. The apostles would flee when the guards came to arrest Jesus. A new people would emerge through them after Jesus had gathered them again

14:28. Jesus promised he would go before the disciples to Galilee. Although they would abandon Jesus in the Garden of Gethsemane, he would reclaim them. He would lead them as a shepherd who had regathered scattered sheep into one flock.

14:29–31. Peter bragged he would not abandon Jesus even if all the others did. Mark mentioned Peter by name, but the other apostles "were saying the same thing also."

Unit Three: With Jesus on the Way to the Cross

Jesus warned Peter he would deny his Lord before sunrise ("before a rooster crows twice"). The *cock crow* was a name given to the bugle call at the beginning of the fourth watch of the night, about 3:00 a.m. Jesus may have been referring to this but more likely was thinking of a literal rooster crowing at dawn. The stress falls not on the time of the denial but on its certainty.

Focusing on the Meaning

Every disciple is vulnerable to failing Jesus. Each of the Twelve wondered whether he were the one who would betray Jesus. Mark singled out Judas and Peter by name, but all were vulnerable.

Judas betrayed his friend Jesus. We can only guess at Judas's reasons. Does simple curiosity cause us to seek more information? Or could something more significant be prompting us? Could it be that in our asking we are trying to distance ourselves from Judas? If we could pinpoint his motives, then we could assure ourselves that his reasons would never affect us. In letting down our defenses, we might easily forsake Jesus for our own reasons.

Peter and the others insisted they would not desert their Lord. Could it be that their brashness was a means to cover their own insecurities and fears? Could it be that their boastfulness prevented them from finding in Jesus the strength to resist the temptation to deny him? Could our pride lead to our forsaking him?

Stressing Christian fellowship offers one means to increase our devotion. We can find strength to remain faithful to Jesus in the new covenant Jesus inaugurated. His death was a unique sacrifice and one that never needs to be repeated. What disciples need now is to break bread and share it in fellowship. There in the presence of Christ they will find support. Sharing one cup means sharing in Christ's future.

Christ's presence is found in the community of faith. Disciples experience the real presence of Christ in observing the Lord's Supper. Different traditions assert that the real presence of Christ is present in different ways at the supper. But all affirm the Lord's presence. Celebrate the Lord's presence.

Seek Christ's presence in different ways. We tend to use spiritual disciplines that stress solitude—prayer, Bible study, meditation. We need to look beyond the individual disciplines and look for Christ's presence in corporate disciplines such as congregational worship and celebration, confession, and serving others, both inside and outside the church.

TEACHING PLANS

Teaching Plan—Varied Learning Activities

Connect with Life

1. Display a bottle of perfume, or show a photograph of expensive perfume from a magazine ad. Discuss how much it costs. Ask, *If you owned this, what would cause you to pour it all out for someone?* Allow time for answers. Say, *We can hardly imagine such an act of devotion.* Then ask, *More seriously, what would cause you to open a vein and pour out your lifeblood for someone, dying for that person?*

2. Say, *Today's lesson passage shows exactly this kind of radical devotion, but it also shows people who draw back from their commitment to Jesus Christ. Let's see what we can learn about being strong in our faith.*

Guide Bible Study

3. Set the scene for the study of the focal passage by summarizing Mark 14:1–9. Provide a brief explanation by using the information in "Understanding the Context" in this *Teaching Guide* and "Faithfulness in the Midst of Materialism (14:1–11)" in the *Study Guide*.

4. Read Mark 14:12–16. Refer learners to the first paragraph under "Faithfulness in the Face of Fear" in the *Study Guide*. Use the information to recount briefly the events of the Exodus.

   Ask, *What connections do you see between the first Passover story and the events of Jesus' ministry, crucifixion, and resurrection?* Lead the class to brainstorm ideas.

5. Read Mark 14:17–21 while the class listens for how Jesus began to talk about his betrayal. Ask, *Why do you think Mark did not name Judas at this point as the betrayer?* After responses, ask, *Why do you*

THE GOSPEL OF MARK: *Jesus' Works and Words*—Teaching Guide

think each of the disciples began to ask, "Surely not I?" (NIV)? Lead further discussion using questions such as these: *What does "betrayal" mean? Can you think of some examples of betrayal? Have you ever been betrayed by someone? How did it feel? Have you ever betrayed someone?* Finally, ask, *Have you ever betrayed Christ?* Allow time to ponder and respond in silence.

6. Refer the class to the section "Faithfulness in the Gift of Grace (14:22–26)" in the *Study Guide*. Enlist someone to read Mark 14:22–26. Use the information in the *Study Guide* section to explain the bread and the cup referred to in the passage. Provide additional information from "Institution of the Lord's Supper (14:22–25)" in "Bible Comments" in this *Teaching Guide*.

   Then read the small article, "Case Study," in the *Study Guide*, and lead the class to discuss answers to the question.

7. Invite someone to read Mark 14:26–31. Explain that the Greek word in verses 27 and 29 that is usually translated "fall away" is *skandalizō* (from which our word *scandal* comes; pronounced *skan duh LEE dzoh*). The Greek word suggests a trap or snare, or even a stumbling block. Make two columns on a markerboard. Label one "Peter" and the other "Us." Lead the class to brainstorm reasons Peter would be *ensnared* to deny Jesus. Then lead the class to note reasons we ourselves are sometimes *ensnared* to deny Jesus. Answers could include *pride, fear, peer pressure*, and others.

Encourage Application

8. Lead the class to think about and recount for one another memorable Lord's Suppers in which they participated. Allow as many anecdotes as time permits. If the group is larger than twelve, you may want to break into several small groups for this experience of sharing.

9. Lead a discussion with questions such as: *What made these Lord's Supper experiences so memorable? What is the purpose of the Lord's Supper?* Encourage the class to think especially of experiences in which they felt their lives were somehow changed. Conclude by stating that one of the purposes of the Lord's Supper is to help Christians remember Jesus' sacrifice as they recommit themselves to their faith. Close with a prayer of commitment or recommitment to Christ.

LESSON 12: Not Me

Teaching Plan—Lecture and Questions

Connect with Life

1. Before class, write this question on the board: *What do you think of when you think of the Lord's Supper?* Begin the class by referring to the question and calling for responses. Follow by asking these questions: *Why do Christians observe the Lord's Supper? What are some other terms Christians use for the Lord's Supper?* List the answers, which should include *communion, Eucharist,* and others. Ask, *What do these different terms mean or suggest?* (Note that the literal meaning for *Eucharist* is *thanksgiving.*)

2. State that this lesson will examine the events and personalities in Mark's account of Jesus' Last Supper. It will give us an opportunity to evaluate how faithful we are as disciples and how the Lord's Supper can encourage us in faithful discipleship.

Guide Bible Study

3. Read Mark 14:1–11. Before the reading, ask the class to listen for the contrasting actions of the people who are mentioned. Point out the contrast between the woman's selfless act on one hand and on the other hand the chief priests and scribes seeking to kill Jesus plus Judas's betraying Jesus for money. Ask, *When is the last time that your love for Jesus inspired you to do something extravagant and sacrificial?* Then ask, *When have you allowed your selfish plans or your desire for material goods to lead you away from doing what honored God?* Allow silent answers.

4. Read Mark 14:12–16. Present a brief lecture about Passover, using information from the *Study Guide* section "Faithfulness in the Face of Fear" and "Bible Comments" in this *Teaching Guide.* Stress the symbolic nature of the traditional Passover celebration. Refer to Exodus 12:21–27. Ask, *Why do you think God instructed the Israelites to do this? What is the result of remembering God's faithful works on a regular basis?*

THE GOSPEL OF MARK: *Jesus' Works and Words*—Teaching Guide

5. Read Mark 14:22–25. Call for volunteers to read Exodus 24:3–8 and Jeremiah 31:31–34. Use the information in "Faithfulness in the Gift of Grace (14:22–26)" in the *Study Guide* and "Bible Comments" in this *Teaching Guide* to explain the meaning of what Jesus did in these verses. Ask, *What are some ways we interpret or understand the use of the bread and the cup in our Lord's Supper celebrations?*

6. Read Mark 14:26–31. Notice the emphasis in Jesus' words of verse 30 and compare them to Peter's emphatic words in verses 29, 31. Ask, *Why do you think Peter was so emphatic about his faithfulness to Jesus?* Invite responses. Follow by asking, *When have we been as emphatic— and failed as thoroughly—in our good intentions to honor and serve Jesus?* Allow time for private reflection.

Encourage Application

7. State that all of us are as vulnerable as Peter to denying our faith in Jesus. Ask, *What are some strategies Christians can use to avoid failures in their faith?* Accept as many answers as are forthcoming. Then stress that just as the Passover was intended for Jews to remember actively God's faithful deliverance from Egyptian slavery, the Lord's Supper can help us remember actively Jesus' sacrifice and the new covenant he inaugurated for those who believe in him. Refer to question 4 in the *Study Guide*, and invite responses.

8. Read 1 Corinthians 11:23–29 as the class follows in their Bibles. Call attention to verses 26–29. Lead the class in silent, prayerful reflection to: (1) confess any sins that make them unworthy of sharing the Lord's cup; (2) thank God for the Christian fellowship inherent in sharing the Lord's Supper; and (3) commit or recommit to faithful discipleship to Christ.

Focal Text
Mark 14:61b–64; 15:9–24, 37–41; 16:1–8

Background
Mark 14:32—16:8

Main Idea
We can trust in and follow Jesus as the crucified yet victorious Son of God because of his resurrection.

Question to Explore
How does Jesus' crucifixion and resurrection affect your life?

Teaching Aim
To lead the class to affirm or re-affirm their trust in Jesus as the crucified yet victorious Son of God

UNIT THREE

With Jesus on the Way to the Cross

Lesson Thirteen
The Worst and Best of Times

BIBLE COMMENTS

Understanding the Context

Mark's Gospel possesses one of the characteristics of a good symphony. Themes are introduced and developed, and then they reappear at a later time. Topics Mark introduced earlier reach a climax during Jesus' last hours on earth.

If the events of the final chapters of Mark sound familiar as you read them, it may be because Jesus had predicted three times that he would suffer, die, and be raised. He was not surprised by what happened. We may view these events as senseless tragedy, as the worst of times. He saw them as completing God's redemption for humanity, the best of times.

Jesus faced the worst hours of his life alone. The disciples abandoned him, despite their protests that they would remain faithful. He prepared himself for his anguish by taking Peter, James, and John to the Garden of Gethsemane to pray. But while Jesus prayed, they slept.

A group of religious leaders and their guards, led by Judas, found Jesus in the Garden. The fallen disciple betrayed him with a kiss, the greeting of friends. The chief priests seized Jesus as the disciples fled.

The Sanhedrin assembled quickly for a sham of a trial. False witnesses testified against Jesus, but they could not agree. Conviction required that at least two witnesses offer the same evidence (Deuteronomy 19:15).

Interpreting the Scriptures

Jesus Before the Court (14:61–64)

14:61–62. The high priest directly questioned Jesus under oath when the witnesses could not agree. Jesus remained silent. He would answer, but only when he was ready.

Mark's Gospel reached a climax when the high priest asked Jesus: "Are You the Christ, the Son of the Blessed One?" The reader has known since Mark 1:1 that the answer to the question is *yes*. The words "Blessed One" mean God. The disciples knew the answer. Peter had affirmed it at Caesarea Philippi (Mark 8:29).

Jesus had accepted both titles when applied to him by others but had consistently prohibited people from using them publicly (see lesson eight on Mark 8:30). Here for the first time, Jesus publicly admitted he was the Messiah. His answer reflected Psalm 110:1 and Daniel 7:13. Both of these verses are Messianic. The answer may refer to Jesus' Second Coming, his resurrection, or both. What Jesus emphasized was his enthronement and exaltation that would follow his suffering. To sit "at the right hand" was to occupy an important and prominent place. "Power" means *mighty one* and was used here for God.

14:63–64. Jesus' answer sealed his fate. The high priest tore his clothes, expressing outrage at Jesus' so-called blasphemy. No more witnesses were needed. Jesus had confessed to being the Messiah and Son of God. For that, Jesus would be condemned. "Blasphemy" could be anything that diminished God's power and majesty. Jesus' claim clearly qualified as blasphemy for the Jews, for it implied he possessed divine authority. Blasphemy was punishable by death (Leviticus 24:16).

Deliberations ceased. The verdict was announced. The Jewish leaders would take Jesus to Pilate to obtain a warrant for his execution.

Jesus Before Pilate (15:9–20)

Pilate was in Jerusalem because of the crowds associated with Passover. His interrogation revealed Jesus posed no threat to Rome. He recognized Jesus' innocence and looked for a way to release Jesus while still appeasing the religious leaders.

Apparently the governor regularly released a prisoner during the Passover celebration. The crowd pressed Pilate to release the rebel Barabbas, who ironically more closely resembled the Jewish image of the Messiah than did Jesus.

15:9–11. Pilate pressed back, asking the crowd ("them") whether they wanted him to free "the King of the Jews." Using this title annoyed those who sought Jesus' death, for they would never refer to Jesus as king. Pilate also knew a major reason for their convicting Jesus was because they resented Jesus' influence with the people. The authorities quickly stirred the crowd into a frenzy, convincing the mob to ask Pilate to free Barabbas.

15:12–14. Pilate still sought to let Jesus go without provoking a riot. He could ill afford for Rome to hear of a large disturbance in Jerusalem. If he freed Barabbas, what was he to do with Jesus? He had determined Jesus was innocent. Maybe the crowd would relent and let him release Jesus too. The crowd shouted for Pilate to crucify Jesus. Pilate proclaimed Jesus' innocence yet again as the crowd continued to push for Jesus' execution. Pilate asked the crowd to name Jesus' crime. They yelled louder for his execution.

15:15. A pacified crowd was more important to Pilate than justice. His weakness of character and his weak political situation were both revealed as he authorized Jesus' execution. He commanded Jesus to be crucified to please the Jews, although he knew Jesus was blameless.

Pilate ordered that Jesus be scourged before sending him off to be crucified. This scourging was much severer than that administered by the Jews. The Jewish punishment was limited to forty lashes. Roman scourging had no limits. Pieces of metal, bone, glass, and sharp rocks were embedded in the leather straps of the whip. Bones were often ripped from a person's back. Death among those being scourged was not uncommon. Then the governor "handed ... over" Jesus for crucifixion.

15:16. The soldiers took Jesus to an inner courtyard ("palace," "Praetorium") before taking him to be crucified. "Cohort" refers to troops stationed in Jerusalem. They were not necessarily Romans and might have been enlisted from conquered territories in the areas surrounding Judea. They had no personal attachment to or concern for a Jewish criminal.

15:17–18. The soldiers found an old purple coat to drape around Jesus. They placed a crown of thorns on his head. The setting suggests this crown was intended more to mock Jesus than inflict pain. Then they hailed Jesus as "King of the Jews." Their ridicule of Jesus was probably directed as much at the Jews as at Jesus.

15:19–20. They repeatedly beat Jesus with a stick ("reed"). Spitting demonstrates the depth of their scorn. They mockingly knelt and bowed before Jesus. The taunting ended as they replaced the "purple robe" with Jesus' clothing. The journey to the cross began.

Jesus at Golgotha (15:21–24, 37–41)

15:21. Condemned criminals carried their own crossbeam to the place of execution. Jesus was so weakened from the flogging he could not do so. The Romans drafted a man named Simon to carry the cross for him. Simon was from Cyrene in North Africa. It appears he was living in the area surrounding Jerusalem. He was entering the city ("coming from the country") as the death squad left the city. Mark may have mentioned Alexander and Rufus because they were known by the church at Rome, the church for which many believe Mark's Gospel was written (see Romans 16:13).

15:22. The death squad arrived at "Golgotha," the place of execution. Golgotha was located outside but near the city walls. The number of people who mocked Jesus at the site suggests it was on a busy road.

Several suggestions have been offered to explain why it was called the "Place of a Skull." (1) It resembled a bald skull. (2) It was located at a place where rock formations resembled sunken eye sockets, hence a skull. (3) It was a place of death.

15:23. Jewish tradition helps identify "they," for it describes a group of women who offered victims of crucifixion a pain-numbing drink. Both "wine" and "myrrh" have this quality. Jesus refused the drink, probably to face this moment in full control of his faculties.

15:24. The soldiers nailed Jesus to the cross and gambled for what meager possessions he had (see Psalm 22:18). Crucifixion was one of the most torturous forms of execution ever devised. Death came slowly, usually by suffocation. Only the most notorious Romans citizens were subject to crucifixion. To have Jesus crucified was to liken him to the most despicable of criminals.

15:37. Jesus had hung on the cross for six hours when he cried out and died (see 15:25, 34). John's Gospel describes this as a cry of completion and triumph: "It is finished!" (John 19:30). Mark portrays the strength Jesus could muster after prolonged suffering.

15:38–39. Two independent actions stressed that something exceptional had happened on the cross. The first event was the tearing of the veil of the temple from top to bottom. The significance of this event is clear although the specific reference is not. The rending of the veil symbolized the ending of the worship of God at the temple and the opening of a different way to God through Christ and his death.

The temple had two veils. One separated the first inner room, the holy place, from the outside courtyard. The second curtain separated the holy place from the holy of holies, the innermost room of the sanctuary. Mark probably meant the latter. This supernatural event symbolized that Christ's death opened access to God to anyone at any time.

The second event was the centurion's declaration: "Truly this man was the Son of God." Interpreters debate whether this statement expressed true belief or whether it meant nothing more than calling Jesus a divine hero or great man. The Roman soldier had observed something special about how Jesus died. While we cannot be certain of the centurion's meaning, Mark used his words to further his purpose: to demonstrate that Jesus was the Son of God.

15:40–41. A group of women who had helped provide for Jesus during his Galilean ministry witnessed his crucifixion. They were witnesses to Jesus' death and burial.

UNIT THREE: With Jesus on the Way to the Cross

Women at the Empty Tomb (16:1–8)

16:1–3. The women purchased spices on Saturday night ("when the Sabbath was over"). That they would anoint a body that had been in the grave for two nights expressed deep devotion. They approached the tomb soon after dawn, wondering how they would remove the stone that covered its entrance.

16:4–5. When the women arrived, they saw the stone had been rolled away. They entered the tomb and discovered a man dressed in white, usually identified as an angel. "White" suggests brilliance (see Mark 9:3, where a similar expression is used).

16:6. The messenger sought to calm the women's fears. He told them Jesus had been raised from the dead. The place they had laid him was empty.

16:7. The angel sent the women to tell the disciples, especially Peter, that Jesus would meet them in Galilee. He mentioned Peter by name because Peter was singled out in his denial of Jesus. Jesus would re-gather his followers in Galilee and restore them after they had fallen away.

16:8. The women obviously obeyed the angel and reported to the disciples, or we would not know their story. They did not act immediately. Mark's Gospel abruptly ends with them telling no one because they were afraid.

Scholars have offered many explanations for this ending and why later writers added other endings to the Gospel. No explanation is without problems, and none has received universal acceptance.

Focusing on the Meaning

We struggle to choose Jesus' way from many options. We know something is wrong with our world. The crowd's choice of Barabbas over Jesus illustrates that many people feel using force can solve our problems. Jesus was killed because the world could not see its true need or accept him as its true king. We want a warrior to deliver us.

Mark understood Jesus to be King. He is hailed as King twice. The crowds welcomed Jesus to Jerusalem the Sunday before his crucifixion. The soldiers mocked Jesus as king before crucifying him. Neither the crowd nor the soldiers understood what it meant for Jesus to be King. But despite their misunderstandings, Mark used these events to assert that Jesus was the messianic King.

Jesus offers another concept of overcoming what is wrong in our world: radical obedience to the will of God. Jesus' obedience brought him into direct conflict with the religious and political establishment. The world's ways were and are *me first*. We fight to preserve what we deem to be our rights. We fight to keep what belongs to us. Jesus' death shows that the way of discipleship leads to a cross. The resurrection shows God prefers Christ's way of serving others. We find life in our death to self.

We must live with ambiguity, confusion, and uncertainty in our Christian journey. I admit I'm perplexed and frustrated by the ending to Mark's Gospel. I like happy endings. I like to tie up all the loose ends.

One interpretation suggests Mark intentionally ended the Gospel this way to leave the story open-ended. Jesus' story did not end with crucifixion or even the resurrection. Jesus' story continues in the life and work of his disciples. Jesus promised to meet the gathered disciples in Galilee. They had failed him in Jerusalem but would continue his work after the resurrection.

The opening word's of Mark's Gospel are "the beginning of the gospel of Jesus Christ." The ending of Mark's Gospel illustrates his opening words. The Gospel of Mark has a beginning, but it does not have an ending. The good news of Jesus is a never-ending story. Even the resurrection does not end the story, for Christ's work continues in his church, in you and me.

We may live in the worst of times. Continuing Christ's work makes possible the best of times.

TEACHING PLANS

Teaching Plan—Varied Learning Activities

Connect with Life

1. State that some people today claim the NASA moon walks in the 1960s were hoaxes and never happened. Also, some people claim the Holocaust never happened. Ask, *What kind of evidence would you*

The Gospel of Mark: Jesus' Works and Words—Teaching Guide

provide in an attempt to show the events did occur? (Suggestions might include newspaper accounts at the time, later books and other documents, eyewitness testimony, and the changes in the lives of people who experienced these events.) Jot the answers on the markerboard. Keep a limit on the amount of discussion.

2. Say, *Today we're going to talk about the death and resurrection of Jesus of Nazareth. Although few people will dispute Jesus' crucifixion, some people claim his resurrection never happened. Each of us can read the accounts and examine our own beliefs.*

Guide Bible Study

3. Review the incidents in Mark 14:32–54—Jesus in the Garden of Gethsemane, Judas's betrayal, and Jesus' arrest.

4. Read Mark 14:61–64. Ask, *Has anyone ever appeared before a judge, even for a traffic violation? How did you feel—brave, intimidated, cocky?* Invite responses. Include comments from people who work within the judicial system, such as attorneys.
    Reread Pilate's question in Mark 14:61 and Jesus' words in Mark 14:62. Note that Jesus was essentially pleading guilty to the (trumped-up) charge of blasphemy, or insulting God. Ask, *How do you imagine Jesus as he said these words? Why do you think Jesus spoke with so much courage and conviction?*

5. Read or briefly recount the incidents of Mark 14:65–72.

6. Divide the class into two groups. Assign Mark 15:1–20 to group one and Mark 15:21–36 to group two. Distribute pencil and paper, or markers and markerboard space. Instruct each group to review the text and note how many groups or individuals insulted, mocked, injured, or otherwise abused Jesus. (Form additional groups and give duplicate assignments if necessary to have groups of six or fewer people.) Call for reports. Ask, *What do you learn from Jesus' reaction of patient, courageous silence and endurance in the face of this horrific treatment?*

7. Enlist someone to read Mark 15:37–47 while the class listens for what Jesus said and how various people responded to Jesus' crucifixion. Using the same groups as in step 6, assign Mark 15:37–41 to

Lesson 13: The Worst and Best of Times

the first and Mark 15:42–47 to the second. This time, instruct the groups to identify how people in their assigned Scripture responded. Call for reports. Ask, *Why would these acts have required immense courage?*

8. Note that Mark's Gospel does not mention the presence of any of the Twelve at the crucifixion. Divide into two groups. (If your class includes both men and women, make one group men and the other group women.) Direct one group to portray the disciples, and the other group the women who followed Jesus. Each group should role play deciding whether to go to the crucifixion or not.

9. Continue in small groups. Read Mark 16:1–8. Say, *One reason the Gospel of Mark is highly credible as a historical document is that it presents unvarnished views of events and of Jesus' closest associates. Pretend your group is a team of Hollywood scriptwriters who wish to portray people in these verses in the most positive light. How would you rewrite Mark 16:1–8?* Allow time for creativity, and then call for readings.

Encourage Application

10. Refer to the list from step 1. Ask, *Do we possess any of these kinds of evidence for Jesus' resurrection? What would we add to the list of evidence?*

11. Refer the class to the "Case Study" in the *Study Guide*. Break into small groups for discussion. Encourage each person to formulate a personal answer. Suggest that each group try role play, with one member as a Jew, one as a Muslim, and one as a Christian. After several minutes to work through the exercise, ask the groups whether they learned anything they want to share with the whole class.

12. Lead the class to reflect on and then comment on the meaning of Jesus' crucifixion and resurrection for their lives. Conclude with prayer for deeper understanding and assurance of God's gracious miracle of the resurrection.

The Gospel of Mark: *Jesus' Works and Words*—Teaching Guide

Teaching Plan—Lecture and Questions

Connect with Life

1. Think of a famous person, living or dead, with whom your class is probably familiar. (This person should not be someone personally known to any class members. Try to avoid using a controversial figure, too.) You might bring a biography or a photograph as a visual aid. Ask, *What are a few things you know about this person?* Be prepared to offer some facts or anecdotes to stimulate other answers.

    Ask, *Does anyone "know" this person? What does it mean to "know" someone?*

2. Say, *We often know about other people, without knowing them personally. In other words, we do not have any sort of relationship with them. As believers in Jesus Christ, however, we can "know" Jesus in a personal way because of the resurrection. In today's lesson, we will review the trial, crucifixion, death, and resurrection of Jesus. We will see how Jesus' triumph over death gives each believer hope and courage.*

Guide Bible Study

3. Review the incidents in Mark 14:32–54. Then enlist someone to read Mark 14:61–64. Explain these verses briefly, using information in "Bible Comments" in this *Teaching Guide*. Ask, *Why do you think Jesus responded as he did in Mark 14:62? How else might he have answered?* Stress that Jesus demonstrated courage and conviction, and in a way he controlled this trial by foreshortening the proceedings.

4. Read or briefly recount the incidents of Mark 14:65—15:8. Then invite someone to read Mark 15:9–24. Explain these verses briefly, using information in "Bible Comments" in this *Teaching Guide*. Follow with questions such as these:

    - Can you think of some ways we choose Barabbas instead of Jesus?
    - Mark 15:16–20 makes clear the soldiers were mocking Jesus, even though they were treating him as one would a king. Can you think of some ways Christians mock Jesus, even though they are practicing orthodox religion?

- Why do you think people would repeat a tragic story such as Jesus' crucifixion? Can you think of modern or personal examples in which this kind of story is repeated? (One example is September 11, 2001.)

5. Call on someone to read Mark 15:37–39. Ask, *Why do you think Mark included the details of these amazing phenomena?*

6. Read Mark 15:40–41. Note that Mark's Gospel does not mention the presence of any of the Twelve at the crucifixion. Ask, *Why do you think the women were present but the disciples likely were not?* Ask, *Are there times in our lives when we face appalling circumstances and react like the women and/or like the disciples? What can we learn from the courage of the women?*

7. Read 16:1–8. Ask, *What would you conclude about the story of Jesus if this was all the information we had? Would you feel encouraged? perplexed?* After a few minutes of discussion, refer to the small article, "The Ending of the Gospel of Mark," in the *Study Guide*. Ask, *How do these verses at the end of Mark add to your understanding—or confusion—about the abrupt ending of the Gospel?*

Encourage Application

8. State that at some time or another, all people have concerns that may seem hopeless (such as health, finances, wayward children, relationships, loneliness, death, and so on). Ask, *Which of these troubles your own heart? Does having someone in your life who cares about you help when you are dealing with these kinds of concerns? How?*

   Then ask, *How can your assurance that Jesus Christ rose from the dead help you have faith, hope, and courage to cope or deal with these concerns?* Allow for private reflection, or break into small groups or pairs.

9. End by singing or reading the words to the hymn, "Because He Lives."[1]

NOTES

1. Words by Gloria Gaither and William J. Gaither. *The Baptist Hymnal* (Nashville, Tennessee: Convention Press, 1991), no. 407.

Focal Text
Luke 2:1–20

Background
Luke 2:1–20

Main Idea
When we truly understand the meaning of God's sending Jesus, we respond by glorifying and praising God.

Question to Explore
Why does Christ's birth bring such joy?

Teaching Aim
To lead the class to explain the meaning of God's sending Jesus and respond by glorifying and praising God

Christmas Lesson

Glory to God!

BIBLE COMMENTS

Understanding the Context

God is great. God is good. God is majestic and powerful. God has been revealing divine glory since speaking the universe into existence. God has been redeeming humanity since the fall. The Almighty called out one immigrant, Abraham, to bless the world through him and his descendants (Genesis 12:1–3). God sent one person, Moses to deliver a nation of slaves from the most powerful monarch in the world (Exodus 3:10). God pledged to one king, David, to build for him an enduring dynasty (2 Samuel 7:13). God sent one man, Jesus, to the world that through him the world would be saved (John 1:12). Too, John wrote of the Son of God, "And the Word became flesh, and dwelt among us, and we saw His glory, glory as of the only begotten from the Father, full of grace and truth" (John 1:14).

Those who behold divine majesty can glorify and praise God. Angels joined their voices singing praises to God in skies over humble shepherds. Awed shepherds journeyed to Bethlehem under starlit skies to see the Savior. They announced to all what they had seen and heard. Then they returned to their flocks, "glorifying and praising God for all that they had heard and seen" (Luke 2:20).

Examining Luke's account of the nativity will help us understand more fully the significance of Jesus' coming. May we experience that same thrill of the ancient shepherds. Too, may we, 2,000 years later, announce to all what we have seen and heard. Now, let's look and see what they heard.

Interpreting the Scriptures

Joseph Registers in Bethlehem (2:1–5)

2:1. The Savior entered this world at a particular time and place in history. Luke provided details because he wanted to present Jesus as the Savior for all people. "In those days" placed Jesus' birth after John the Baptist's.

Emperor Augustus had ordered that a census be taken of "all the inhabited earth" (literal Greek translation, *all the world*). The phrase was often applied to the Roman Empire. The census was likely for tax registration because Rome exempted Jews from military service. God used this census to bring Joseph and Mary to Bethlehem, where the prophets had foretold the Messiah would be born. God was using the power of the Roman Empire to further the divine plan. We might note also an implied contrast between Roman power and divine power.

2:2. Luke identified the census as the "first" one, which probably means the first one administered by Quirinius. This statement has raised eyebrows regarding Luke's historical accuracy. Jesus' birth occurred before the death of Herod the Great in 4 B.C., but no Roman records have been found that verify a census around that time. Similar registrations occurred at fourteen-year intervals, and one verifiable census is dated in A.D. 6. Historians have discovered that Quirinius commanded Rome's military forces in Syria from about 7–6 B.C. He was not governor but exerted considerable influence. The responsibility for carrying out a census would have fallen on his shoulders. A census at this earlier time is not inconceivable.

2:3. Augustus allowed conquered peoples to maintain native customs as much as possible. A Jew customarily registered in his hometown, even if he had moved elsewhere. The registrant would be expected to provide such information as name, occupation, property, and family.

CHRISTMAS LESSON: Glory to God!

2:4–5. Joseph and Mary made the trip to Bethlehem from Nazareth in Galilee. Bethlehem is located about five miles south of Jerusalem. The trip from Nazareth to Bethlehem normally would take about three days. Bethlehem, which means *house of bread*, was known as the "city of David." David grew up tending sheep in this vicinity (1 Samuel 16:4; 17:15). Joseph went to Bethlehem because he was a descendant of David.

Why Joseph took Mary with him is not stated. It is unlikely she was required to register. Joseph's registration would have included her. He might have taken her to spare her from ridicule in Nazareth from those who were whispering about her pregnancy. Too, they might have been considering moving to Bethlehem. Matthew's Gospel suggests that Joseph and Mary were living in Bethlehem when they fled to Egypt (Matthew 2:8–11,16). Since Mary was traveling with Joseph, many people might have considered them married. Luke noted they were only engaged. The marriage had not been sexually consummated. Another possible reason for Joseph taking Mary was because he wanted to care for her in the latter stages of her pregnancy.

Jesus Is Born (2:6–7)

Mary gave birth to her "firstborn son" and laid him in a manger. The word "firstborn" suggests she had other children later, but it can mean simply that Jesus was her first child with no reference to later children at all. "Firstborn" would also denote the privileges and responsibilities of the eldest son. Mary's wrapping of Jesus herself may suggest she and Joseph were alone at Jesus' birth. Jesus' first crib was a feeding trough for animals because the family could find no lodging in the "inn."

We can only speculate about where Jesus was born. An ancient tradition locates it in a cave just outside the city. Or it may have been in an animal courtyard outside a public inn. Innkeepers used these areas to house poorer guests when rooms were full.

Still another option is the birth happened in a house. Houses in that day often had two levels. The family lived on the upper level. Here they slept, cooked, and ate. The lower level housed animals when necessary. The phrase "no room for them in the inn" would mean the upper level was full. A full house of relatives in town for the census relegated Joseph and Mary to the lower section with the animals.

Each possible site for Jesus' birth suggests that Jesus began his life in the poorest of circumstances, where social barriers had little meaning. The poorest people can feel that the Savior of the world who was laid in the manger came for them, without pretense, without fanfare.

Angels Appear to Shepherds (2:8–14)

2:8–9. In truth, considerable fanfare did accompany Jesus' birth. However, it occurred in an isolated spot and was directed to obscure folks. Shepherds who were watching their flocks on the hills just outside Bethlehem were the first to hear of the Savior's birth.

Shepherds lived on the fringe of society. Jewish society distrusted them, perceiving them to be thieves. Courts would not allow them to testify. Their work made it impossible to maintain ritual purity.

The fields in which the shepherds were staying may have been located between Bethlehem and Jerusalem, the same area where David had tended sheep many years before. The animals these shepherds were watching might end up as sacrificial offerings in the temple. How ironic (and tragic) that the shepherds who tended the sacrificial flocks were barred from offering temple sacrifices.

The shepherds had apparently combined their flocks for mutual protection during the night. The words "keeping watch" indicate vigilance. These shepherds were made of the same stuff as the shepherd boy David, who stated he had killed a lion and a bear to protect his sheep (1 Sam. 17:34–36).

Shepherds did not scare easily. Yet, they cowered when the "glory of the Lord" pierced the night sky, a bright light that reflected the very presence of God (see Exodus 16:10).

2:10–11. "Do not be afraid," said the messenger. (Have you ever noticed how many times in Luke 1—2 an angel says, "Do not be afraid"? See Luke 1:13, 30; 2:10.) "I bring you good news of great joy." The angel had not appeared to destroy them but to herald the birth of a Savior. Joy is one of Luke's recurring themes. This good news was for "all the people." While this phrase normally meant the people of Israel, a wider audience might have been intended at this time.

Of the Gospel writers, only Luke and John used "Savior" (meaning *deliverer;* Luke 1:47; 2:11; John 4:42). Saviors were people who delivered from danger or disease, such as rulers. Ancient deities were called *savior.* To call Jesus Savior affirmed he could deliver when these other entities could not.

CHRISTMAS LESSON: Glory to God!

The angel described the Savior with the double title, "Christ the Lord." "Christ" is the Greek equivalent for the Hebrew word *Messiah* and refers to God's anointed one.

The Greek translation of the Old Testament used the word "Lord" for God. The title also was applied to ancient rulers. An oath of allegiance to the Roman Empire was, "Caesar is Lord." Christians were martyred because they would not repeat these words. For them, Jesus was Lord.

2:12. The angel directed the shepherds to the place where they could find the child, the Savior. What would distinguish this child was his crib, a manger. The shepherds would be welcome in this humble place.

2:13–14. A throng of angels joined the messenger to praise God for the Savior's birth. The song glorified "God in the highest." God had sent peace to earth. Through Christ's birth one can experience genuine peace. Peace means more than absence of conflict. It means harmony with God. Peace sprang up because the Savior brought salvation to this world.

The angels' final chorus called for "peace among men with whom He is pleased" (Luke 2:14). Humanity is the beneficiary of God's pleasure.

The Shepherds Find the Savior (2:15–20)

2:15–16. The shepherds hurried to Bethlehem to search for the child after the angels departed. There they found the family just as the angel had described.

2:17–19. The shepherds told Mary and Joseph what they had witnessed on the hillsides, particularly the statements about the "Child." Mary remembered these words and reflected on them. Perhaps she shared them later with her son and with Luke, who recorded them here.

2:20. The shepherds returned to their fields and to their lives. They had feared the angel's appearance. They had ventured to Bethlehem and seen the Savior for themselves. They had returned, praising God for Jesus' birth and for God's intrusion into their lives and into the world. They were the first human witnesses to Jesus, the Savior, Christ the Lord.

CHRISTMAS LESSON: Glory to God!

Focusing on the Meaning

My family bought a new Christmas tree several years ago, and I lost one of my yuletide tasks. Stringing lights was my job. Replacing the old tree with the new was a bittersweet experience. I enjoyed stringing the lights, but the new tree has twice as many lights. And when it comes to Christmas trees, and Christmas decorations, one can never have too many lights.

The angel appeared to the shepherds surrounded by the brightness of God's dazzling glory. Hosts of angels sang in chorus, "Glory to God in the highest" (2:14). The shepherds reacted by worshiping the newborn Savior by glorifying and praising God.

This Christmas, think lights. Think Savior. Sing praises. Glorify God.

Glorify God because God is great. A virgin conceived and bore a son. A mighty empire's census brought Mary and Joseph to the very place where the prophets had predicted the Christ would be born. God uses the events in this world and in our lives to achieve his purpose. God is in control.

Glorify God because God keeps his word. The Old Testament promised that God would send a Messiah to deliver the people. Jesus was the Christ (*Messiah, anointed one*) God pledged.

Glorify God because God saves. God sent Jesus into our world to redeem the world. The Savior whom the Almighty sent would grow up and teach his disciples that "the Son of Man did not come to be served, but to serve, and to give His life a ransom for many" (Mark 10:45). By his death we are redeemed.

Glorify God because God intrudes in our lives. Life may leave us feeling we are caught on a treadmill. Today looks a whole lot like yesterday. Get up, get dressed, eat breakfast (you should), go to work, go to church (remember I'm a pastor), go to sleep, get up. God sent Jesus to be our Savior to transform us from common existence to purposeful life.

CHRISTMAS LESSON: Glory to God!

TEACHING PLANS

Teaching Plan—Varied Learning Activities

Connect with Life

1. Begin by sharing the memories of the *Study Guide* writer about the best Christmases he remembers. Share with the group your favorite memories of Christmas. Be sure to include Christmases from your childhood, youth, and now as an adult. Emphasize the joy Christmas brought you in the different stages of your life.

2. Hand each group member a card. Instruct them to write the words "Christmas Joy" at the top of the card. Then ask the class to take a few minutes to write a short phrase, draw a picture, or place a word or words that describe the greatest memory of Christmas joy. After a few minutes, invite them to share the different stories and symbols of joy.

3. Before class begins, find a manger and cover it with a cloth that conceals the entire manger. At this point in the lesson, share your Christmas memory and great symbol of joy on any Christmas in your life. Slip the cloth off the manger and say, *Jesus Christ's birth*.

Guide Bible Study

4. Lead the group to reflect on the birth of a special child in their lives. Give an example of how a special birth brought joy into your life. It could be a child, grandchild, or a friend's child. Ask them to remember the joy the child brought to the families and friends. Guide the class through the section "Praise of Obedience: Joseph and Mary (2:1–7)" in the *Study Guide*, which tells the difficulties Mary and Joseph had in getting to the manger. Enlist someone to share the difficulties they or someone else had in the birth of a baby. Invite someone to read Luke 2:7. Refer to the statement about the cloth that wrapped baby Jesus. Before you come to class, tear strips of cloth to resemble the strips that wrapped baby Jesus. Give each member a strip to remember the joy of Jesus' birth.

Christmas Lesson: Glory to God!

5. Divide the group into two or more groups (no more than six people per group). Ask each group to read Luke 2:8–15 and come up with a special announcement of Jesus' birth in a contemporary setting. Tell them to use the message of the angels and the heavenly host as their pattern.

6. Point out that the *Study Guide* compares the shepherds' story in Luke 2:8–20 to a four-act play under the heading "Praise Through Witness: the Shepherds (2:16–20)." Allow the groups from step 5 to role-play the four acts of these verses.

   - Act 1—Watching the sheep (2:8–14)
   - Act 2—The search (2:15)
   - Act 3—The discovery (2:16)
   - Act 4—Share the news (2:17–20)

Wrap up the play by saying, *This is the simple, yet profound, way God announced the birth of his Son to the world. He still uses people to tell other people about his Son and the joy they can have with him in their lives.*

Encourage Application

7. Refer to and summarize the section "Implications and Actions" in the *Study Guide*. Then point out that God started Christmas by giving us the greatest gift, his Son. State: *God gave us a gift that continues to give as we give the gift away to others, our Savior Jesus Christ. We have two responses to a gift like this: glory and praise; and sharing the gift.* Give the members two cards each. Instruct them to write "Thank You" at the top of one card and "A Gift I Give" at the top of the other. Ask them to spend a few moments praying and writing a thank-you card to God for the Savior he gave us at Christmas, Jesus. Ask them to take the second card as a reminder to pray and take some action to share the real joy of Christ with a friend, neighbor, or coworker. Encourage them to keep the cards in their Bibles as a reminder of the best Christmas.

8. Pray, giving God glory and praise for the best Christmas, and ask God to help you to be faithful to share the story of Christmas.

CHRISTMAS LESSON: Glory to God!

Teaching Plan—Lecture and Questions

Connect with Life

1. Invite the class to name some Christmas gifts popular with children. Lead the group to think about each gift and give an opinion as to why they think this gift is popular.

2. After the group has discussed the different gifts, ask them what kind of joy they think the gifts will bring and how long this joy will last. When the evaluation of the gifts and their lasting joy is over, share with them that today's lesson talks about a joy that started more than 2,000 years ago and will last all the way through eternity, Jesus.

Guide Bible Study

3. Share with the group the information in the *Study Guide* under the heading "Praise of Obedience: Mary and Joseph (2:1–7)." Emphasize the topics of *savior vs. true Savior* and *no vacancy*. Use the following questions to guide discussion:

   - How easy was it for people of the day to see Caesar Augustus as the savior of the world as opposed to Jesus, the true Savior?
   - If you were the innkeeper to whom Joseph and Mary came to find a room, what would you have done to accommodate their needs?

4. Enlist someone to read Luke 2:6–7. Ask the group to close their eyes and imagine being at the manger. Allow for a minute or two of silence, and then invite individuals to share their reactions. Help the group to realize the birth of baby Jesus was truly "joy to the world."

5. Invite someone to read Luke 2:8–15. Ask the group to listen for what the angel and the heavenly host did. After the reading of the Scripture, explain the verses by using the information in the *Study Guide* under the heading "Praise of Heaven: the Angels (2:8–15)" and in "Bible Comments" in this *Teaching Guide*. Then ask the group to share what they heard about the angels' activities in this passage and the attitude the angels conveyed. Emphasize the joy the angels brought to Jesus' birth announcement.

CHRISTMAS LESSON: Glory to God!

6. Explain to the group the position of a shepherd in Jesus' time, using information from "Praise Through Witness: the Shepherds (2:16–20)" in the *Study Guide*. Discuss with the group God's choosing common people to spread the news of the birth of the King of kings.

Encourage Application

7. Use the questions in the *Study Guide* to lead the class to respond personally to the Scripture study.

8. Lead the class to discuss the suggestions in "Bringing It Home" in the *Study Guide*.

9. Encourage the group to identify one person with whom they want to share their joy of Christ during the Christmas season. Pray that God will give each person an opportunity to share with boldness the joy of Christ.

10. Close by singing or reading the words to "Joy to the World."[1]

NOTES

1. Words by Isaac Watts. *The Baptist Hymnal* (Nashville, Tennessee: Convention Press, 1991), 87.

CHRISTMAS LESSON: Glory to God!

How to Order More Bible Study Materials

It's easy! Just fill in the following information. For additional Bible study materials, see www.baptistwaypress.org or get a complete order form of available materials by calling 1-866-249-1799 or e-mailing baptistway@bgct.org.

Title of item	Price	Quantity	Cost
This Issue:			
Mark:Jesus' Works and Words—Study Guide (BWP001022)	$2.95		
Mark:Jesus' Works and Words—Large Print Study Guide (BWP001023)	$3.15		
Mark:Jesus' Works and Words—Teaching Guide (BWP001024)	$3.45		
Additional Issues Available:			
Genesis 12—50: Family Matters—Study Guide (BWP000034)	$1.95		
Genesis 12—50: Family Matters—Large Print Study Guide (BWP000032)	$1.95		
Genesis 12—50: Family Matters—Teaching Guide (BWP000035)	$2.45		
Leviticus, Numbers, Deuteronomy—Study Guide (BWP000053)	$2.35		
Leviticus, Numbers, Deuteronomy—Large Print Study Guide (BWP000052)	$2.35		
Leviticus, Numbers, Deuteronomy—Teaching Guide (BWP000054)	$2.95		
Joshua, Judges—Study Guide (BWP000047)	$2.35		
Joshua, Judges—Large Print Study Guide (BWP000046)	$2.35		
Joshua, Judges—Teaching Guide (BWP000048)	$2.95		
1 and 2 Samuel—Study Guide (BWP000002)	$2.35		
1 and 2 Samuel—Large Print Study Guide (BWP000001)	$2.35		
1 and 2 Samuel—Teaching Guide (BWP000003)	$2.95		
Job, Ecclesiastes, Habakkuk, Lamentations: Dealing with Hard Times—Study Guide (BWP001016)	$2.75		
Job, Ecclesiastes, Habakkuk, Lamentations: Dealing with Hard Times—Large Print Study Guide (BWP001017)	$2.85		
Job, Ecclesiastes, Habakkuk, Lamentations: Dealing with Hard Times—Teaching Guide (BWP001018)	$3.25		
Psalms and Proverbs: Songs and Sayings of Faith—Study Guide (BWP001000)	$2.75		
Psalms and Proverbs: Songs and Sayings of Faith—Large Print Study Guide (BWP001001)	$2.85		
Psalms and Proverbs: Songs and Sayings of Faith—Teaching Guide (BWP001002)	$3.25		
Luke: Journeying to the Cross—Study Guide (BWP000057)	$2.35		
Luke: Journeying to the Cross—Large Print Study Guide (BWP000056)	$2.35		
Luke: Journeying to the Cross—Teaching Guide (BWP000058)	$2.95		
The Gospel of John: The Word Became Flesh—Study Guide (BWP001008)	$2.75		
The Gospel of John: The Word Became Flesh—Large Print Study Guide (BWP001009)	$2.85		
The Gospel of John: The Word Became Flesh—Teaching Guide (BWP001010)	$3.25		
Acts: Toward Being a Missional Church—Study Guide (BWP001013)	$2.75		
Acts: Toward Being a Missional Church—Large Print Study Guide (BWP001014)	$2.85		
Acts: Toward Being a Missional Church—Teaching Guide (BWP001015)	$3.25		
Romans: What God Is Up To—Study Guide (BWP001019)	$2.95		
Romans: What God Is Up To—Large Print Study Guide (BWP001020)	$3.15		
Romans: What God Is Up To—Teaching Guide (BWP001021)	$3.45		

1, 2 Timothy, Titus, Philemon—*Study Guide* (BWP000092)	$2.75	_____	_____
1, 2 Timothy, Titus, Philemon—*Large Print Study Guide* (BWP000091)	$2.85	_____	_____
1, 2 Timothy, Titus, Philemon—*Teaching Guide* (BWP000093)	$3.25	_____	_____
Hebrews and James—*Study Guide* (BWP000037)	$1.95	_____	_____
Hebrews and James—*Teaching Guide* (BWP000038)	$2.45	_____	_____
Revelation—*Study Guide* (BWP000084)	$2.35	_____	_____
Revelation—*Large Print Study Guide* (BWP000083)	$2.35	_____	_____
Revelation—*Teaching Guide* (BWP000085)	$2.95	_____	_____

Coming for use beginning March 2008

1 and 2 Kings: Leaders and Followers—*Study Guide* (BWP001025)	$2.95	_____	_____
1 and 2 Kings: Leaders and Followers—*Large Print Study Guide* (BWP001026)	$3.15	_____	_____
1 and 2 Kings: Leaders and Followers—*Teaching Guide* (BWP001027)	$3.45	_____	_____

Standard (UPS/Mail) Shipping Charges*	
Order Value	Shipping charge
$.01—$9.99	$6.00
$10.00—$19.99	$7.00
$20.00—$39.99	$8.00
$40.00—$79.99	$9.00
$80.00—$99.99	$12.00
$100.00—$129.99	$14.00
$130.00—$149.99	$18.00
$150.00—$199.99	$21.00
$200.00—$299.99	$26.00
$300.00 and up	10% of order value

Cost of items (Order value) _____
Shipping charges (see chart*) _____
TOTAL _____

*Plus, applicable taxes for individuals and other taxable entities (not churches) within Texas will be added. Please call 1-866-249-1799 if the exact amount is needed prior to ordering.

Please allow three weeks for standard delivery. For express shipping service: Call 1-866-249-1799 for information on additional charges.

_____

YOUR NAME   PHONE

_____

YOUR CHURCH   DATE ORDERED

_____

MAILING ADDRESS

_____

CITY   STATE   ZIP CODE

MAIL this form with your check for the total amount to
BAPTISTWAY PRESS, Baptist General Convention of Texas,
333 North Washington, Dallas, TX 75246-1798
(Make checks to "Baptist Executive Board.")

OR, **FAX** your order anytime to: 214-828-5376, and we will bill you.

OR, **CALL** your order toll-free: 1-866-249-1799
(M-Th 8:30 a.m.-8:30 p.m.; Fri 8:30 a.m.-5:00 p.m. central time),
and we will bill you.

OR, **E-MAIL** your order to our internet e-mail address:
baptistway@bgct.org, and we will bill you.

OR, **ORDER ONLINE** at www.baptistwaypress.org.

We look forward to receiving your order! Thank you!